JEAN BRUCHESI
of The Royal Society of Canada

CANADA

THE RYERSON PRESS, Toronto
and
FERNAND NATHAN, Paris

TABLE OF CONTENTS

CANADA

A T the time that the French navigator, Jacques Cartier, was sailing up the St. Lawrence River (1535), Canada — a word of Iroquois origin meaning "group of huts" — signified only that country which lay between the two modern cities of Quebec and Three Rivers. Later, following discoveries, the name, together with that of New France, served to designate all of the land explored by the French from Labrador to the head of the Great Lakes (1). The very name of New France was attributed by the author of the first (1611) of the famous Jesuit *Relations*, to "the lands and territories of America, or of the West Indies, which lie on the other side of the Guyenne Ocean to the West." And why was this country called New France? Still writing the missionary stated "because those lands are parallel with the land of our France, divided by the one and only Western Sea", and moreover because "this country was firstly discovered by the French Bretons in 1504".

As a result of the Treaty of Paris (1763), whereby France abandoned all claim to Canada and its dependencies in behalf of England, half of a continent became English. Twelve years had hardly elapsed when the thirteen former British colonies threw off the yoke of London. Notwithstanding difficulties, they carried on until their borders were extended to the shores of the Pacific. The Northern regions were not to be disdained. But England was on

---

(1) In fact, New France comprised all the land in North America which had been discovered and colonized by the French.

guard, and when the hour struck during the second half of the nineteenth century, Canada in turn, extended from ocean to ocean.

Today, with the exception of Mexico and Danish Greenland, North America is divided into two countries. The largest area is not covered by the American Republic, including Alaska, but, by Canada whose name designates a territory as vast as that of Europe, which measures 3,610,000 square miles. Almost half of this territory comprises productive lands, agricultural and wooded. The balance consists of waste land more or less inhabitable. Fresh water is plentiful everywhere, and lakes, streams and rivers cover a surface which represents 6 % of the total area.

Compared with Europe, Canada offers few possibilities which are not within the reach of man. Its only neighbour is the United States, from which it is separated by a hardly perceptible frontier of 4,200 miles in length. Some lakes, owing to their size, seem to be real inland seas, such as Lake Superior, Great Bear Lake, and Lake Winnipeg. A third of its territory contains nothing but forests. The entrance to the Gulf of St. Lawrence is some 1,200 miles from Montreal, and yet 26,000 ton ships may safely penetrate far inland; and without leaving Canadian waters, heavy cargoes may even cover 2,400 miles, that is, the distance between the Strait of Belle Isle and the western head of Lake Superior. From the end of November to the middle of April, the St. Lawrence, one of the most important roads "which move along", navigable through its whole length, and whose history is that of Canada, is partly covered with ice and therefore closed to navigation; but Montreal has become one of the chief harbours in the world. The largest extent of land is uninhabited owing to the nature of the soil and climate; but Canada ranks third or fourth among the commercial powers of the world. Regions such as Nova Scotia, the Valley of the St. Lawrence and that of Ontario, not to mention the Western Prairies, are remarkably fertile; however, there are vast spaces of barren land. Millions could inhabit this country, eighteen times the size of France, which barely contains over fifteen million people, nine-tenths of whom are established at a distance of not more than 200 miles from the American border.

It is universally acknowledged that history is the determining factor of the Canadian state and of the Canadian people. Yet it cannot be denied that geography, unaffected by politics, has influenced the very course of this history. It has in fact — though Canada was erected, under certain aspects, in opposition to its laws — caused the country to be divided into very distinct regions in accordance with the nature of the soil or subsoil, and climatic conditions. Therefore, these regions are so neatly separated one from the other, that one wonders, at times, if Canada is not, to some extent, a geographical "absurdity" as well as a political one. It is true that geographers do not always agree as to the number of regions into which the immense territory is divided; nevertheless they do agree on the exact limits of each one. On the other hand, it is none the less true that the genius of man has succeeded in overcoming obstacles which had been considered, up to now, as insuperable. Indeed is there not reason to be astonished that Canada, contrary to the greater number of countries, does not present a picture of true national or economic unity. Furthermore, as it does not enjoy true national unity, it is not a country which is easily known or understood.

Canadian soil has undergone numerous and great changes. The slow action of the glaciers finished up by levelling summits and sinking rivers and lakes. Traces of this action are particularly apparent in the most extensive of the five geographical regions : that which is covered by the Canadian Shield, which includes all the northern part of the Provinces of Quebec, Ontario, Manitoba and Saskatchewan, from Labrador to the Mackenzie River, and from Lake Superior to the Arctic, and is, 2,500,000 square miles or 65 % of the entire area. This immense rocky territory comprises little arable land. Characterized by low hills, it abounds with lakes, rivers, swamps and forests, and contains enormous metal deposits.

Beginning with the east, the second region is that of the Maritime Provinces, which groups together Nova Scotia, New Brunswick, Prince Edward Island, and, since 1949, Newfoundland. Partly mountainous, largely wooded, it is relatively fit for cultivation though infinitely less than that of the third region : the Valley of the St. Lawrence and that of the Great Lakes. Owing to the climate, which is less severe than elsewhere, and the abundant forestry, mineral, hydraulic and agricultural resources, this region is undoubtedly the most important one in Canada. Therein lives 60 % of the population, and its industrial activity is estimated as having an output equal to at least three quarters of the total production of the country.

This industrial activity tends however, though imperceptibly, to move westwards. Whatever the number of oil wells in Alberta may be it is still the wheat fields of Manitoba and Saskatchewan that remain, together with their breeding centres, the chief characteristic and primary source of wealth of the Central Plain or the Prairies. Up to now at least, the extreme western region — the Rocky Mountains and British Columbia — ranks third, after Ontario and Quebec, insofar as the volume of industrial production is concerned. A mountainous country where agriculture is of a minor importance, where even the fisheries along the Pacific Coast give way to the forest and mines, and whose climate, in the southern part at least, is milder than anywhere else in the country.

Thus appears the physical Canada in the eyes of a man of the twentieth century, henceforth fixed it seems, within the frame which nature has outlined for it, between three oceans and the United States. Thus Canada appeared, on a lower scale though, in the eyes of those who landed to the east, four centuries ago. "The land God gave Cain", wrote Cartier on sighting Labrador; and John Davis, the explorer who reached Hudson Bay in 1587, saw neither tree nor grass, but only ice which covered "the sea as far as two leagues from the shore". Strictly speaking, this dreary picture of bleak areas, swept by polar winds, was that of the Great North. Nor has there been any change in the region lying between the Davis and Alaska Straits, where the climate remains very severe. But today man is informed as to the extent of mineral wealth concealed under rock and snow, and of which he has undertaken the development. He has been known to even cultivate, here and there, plots of ungrateful soil, when not enjoying the modern comforts of meteorological stations or those of the counters of the Hudson's Bay Company, in the North West Territories and the Yukon. A wild country perhaps, but only to a certain degree, and especially not in the sense of that which is applied to certain regions of Africa, Asia or South America. The population consists of a handful of white men — 13,000 — a number equal to that of Indians and Eskimos, whose primitive ways of living, in the Island of the Arctic Archipelago at least, are in opposition to those of modern life which brush them by through the double sign of airplane and radio.

But to the south, from the Atlantic to the Pacific, the scene is quite different. The country is no longer "an endless forest", as at the time of the first settlers, and the lands are "as rich as those of France". Therefore, it is advisable as of yore "to avoid the illusion by which so many have been unwittingly misled" : that of believing that by the mere fact of setting foot on Canadian soil, a fortune is gained.

NEW FRANCE

The discovery of America realized, in part only, the dream of the men of the Middle Ages, who had long been drawn by the mystery of the lands beyond the Mediterranean. America was not an objective in itself. Once recognized as a new continent, it became an obstacle which barred the way to the East and which had to be by-passed should it not contain the gold that was needed by Spain, Portugal, England and France. Suddenly the Atlantic assumed a vast importance — which it has kept to this day but for other reasons — and rival powers hastened to embark on its waters.

France forever seeking "to expand beyond her borders", according to the very words of the historian, Gabriel Hanotaux, was not in the least eager to undertake the quest for a route across the Atlantic to reach the land of spices and precious metals. Vikings, Breton fishermen, Normans and Basques had known the route to Newfoundland for some time past, when Verrazano, an Italian, following in the footsteps of John and Sebastian Cabot, undertook to explore the American shores at the request of Francis I. Neither he nor the others were the true founders. This title justly belongs to Jacques Cartier, a Frenchman from "Saint-Malo of the Isle in Brittany", for having really discovered Canada.

On the twenty-fourth day of July, 1534, on a Gaspé headland, there was raised a cross which towered thirty-feet above the earth. The men who planted it there were subjects of the King of France, and it was in his name, that they took possession of a land of which no man yet determined the boundaries or estimated the value of its resources. These men were Christians; their captain was devout, and their country, whose territory they were peacefully extending, was the "eldest daughter of the Church". If they could not properly be called missionaries and, still less, apostles, they yet understood, or Cartier understood for them, that sixteenth century France could have appeared in the New World in no more noble guise. The Indians who surrounded the kneeling mariners grasped nothing of the symbolism of the scene of which they were the astonished witnesses; but the Frenchmen knew that to take possession of the land in this manner was to give a promise for the future. For the moment, what else could France do, occupied as she was with maintaining her continental unity? Indeed, after ascertaining that Canada's wealth was not in precious metals but in pelts, she put off till later the task of colonizing far-away lands. Thus Canada had hardly emerged from the light of history when it withdrew into the shadows again, and work of French expansion was halted the moment it began. Halted only, and not destroyed forever, for when peace returned to France again under the white plume of Henri IV, there were those who remembered that French civilization had been the first to be implanted in North America, and that a sailor of Saint-Malo had one day borne far into the interior of the land, as far as the Island of Hochelaga, the cross and the lilies of France.

At the end of the sixteenth century, efforts at colonization were resumed. The hey-day of the fisheries was past, even though fish continued, and would continue, to be, if not a source of wealth, at least a means of earning the daily bread. The fur trade became the wealth-giver of Canada, that which hereafter, in the absence of gold, silver, iron and copper, whose discovery was to come much later, that which was to prove a great barrier in the path of colonization, without however completely preventing the spread of French civilization. It was also to maintain a lengthy and bloody rivalry between the English and French elements. The clearing of land and the pursuit of agriculture were to be neglected, thus undermining in a political sense the permanence of the task. But through it, notwithstanding the violence of the struggle at times, France was to mark with an indelible seal the whole continent of America, saturated with the blood and sweat of her sons.

Less than a century after the advent of Cartier, another Frenchman, Samuel de Champlain, a native of Brouage, in Saintonge, one the noblest figures in French colonial history, founded Quebec in 1608. Through his many voyages of exploration, the accuracy of his sight, together with his visionary qualities and doggedness, Champlain was the true "Father of New France".

Quebec was to serve again for a long time as a stopping place at one end of the dangerous voyages which for a century and a half were to bring to the city, in small groups, governmental officials and soldiers of the King, nuns and missionaries, workers and farmers. To the west, to the south and to the north, great wooded territories offered the lure of the unknown and the bait of treasures which awaited only the hand of man to garner them. For exploration was not a passing whim; it was an imperious need ordained by politics and religious fervour, even though it so happened that many many times it ended up in a mere bartering of goods. While some set forth upon discovery and adventure, extending year by year the boundaries of the Royal domain and the front line of battle where there lay in ambush an enemy of a hundred faces — forest, climate, Indians, the English — others remained behind to assure the protection of the base against the hazards of retreat or defeat.

Such was Champlain's programme when the first settlers arrived, headed by Louis Hébert, a druggist from Paris, who had a reading knowledge of Hebrew, Greek and Latin. For the first time, lands were ploughed, seeds planted and harvests gathered. Then, twenty years after its founding, the English were masters of Canada. Meanwhile, in Paris, among those who were close to the sovereign, there were some, forerunners of the philosophers of the eighteenth century, who believed and said that if France lost the Rock of Quebec, they would lose nothing of great value. Champlain pleaded his cause stubbornly and insistently; and in the end, Richelieu gave in with confidence and realized the importance of Champlain's farsightedness. France could not keep first place among European nations if she was not mistress of the seas, and that she could not be without the possession of distant bases; and Canada was precisely one of these bases. So the impetus was given, timidly at first, but never again would it completely stop, even though there was uncertainty as to whether Versailles would always sustain it. New France was not to be delivered over completely to merchants : it was to become a real colony, a lasting settlement which would reproduce beneath American skies, though with variants, the image of far-off France; which would be another France until it became a different France. Unlike his successors, Champlain's objective was not merely the conquest of a vast territory. He wanted the name of the true God to be known and the Christian religion established : Frenchmen were to till the land, "that they may have there the means of livelihood", and the land "will furnish all that man can wish for his needs or for his pleasure."

The men suitable for Canada were "those who are willing to work and not those who are rich, and desire all the comforts of France". A severe and long winter was not the only obstacle to be overcome, there was also those of perilous crossings, settlement difficulties, and the sly attacks of the Iroquois, which ceased only to be replaced by the struggle with the English. Physical strength was not to be undervalued, nor were moral qualities, as important if not more so, which accounted for the close supervision practised over the colonists in their comings and goings.

For a long time it was believed and repeated that the greater number of these settlers had originated from Normandy. But in reality such was not the case. With the exception of the east and south-east frontier provinces — and even so the Acadians number some Basques among their ancestors — it was the Kingdom of France almost wholly that peopled the American colony, which became Canada, with a slowness which was exasperating at times. In fact, at the time of the first census, in 1666, the population of New France did not number more than 4,000 souls. It increased to a little over 16,000 in 1706, exceeded 34,000 twenty-five years later, and reached about 70,000, including troops, at the time of the conquest. As the fecundity of Canadian families was already notable in the seventeenth and eighteenth centuries, the conclusion is obvious, that immigration was not the principal factor in an increase of population so worthy of praise indeed, but greatly inferior to that it might have been if comparison is made with the population of the English colonies, which went from nothing to over one million in the same period of time. Hardly ten thousand settlers, men, women and children, who were neither social outcasts, orphans, of questionable parentage, nor returned convicts, settled in Canada between 1608 and 1736.

With great difficulty and even heroically at times, those who came cultivated the land; and this work was to be a hard struggle for a long time. Both men and women unceasingly carried out the desperate task of clearing the land, pushing the forest back from year to year, taking root, so to say, in the land itself, and moulding the country to their own likeness. At first, owing to the very nature of things, the settlers were forced to become architects, carpenters and masons. Later, the craftsmen arrived : masters, journeymen or apprentices soon grouped into guilds, whose taste and feeling were quickly adapted to the climate as well as to the materials of a different world. They had the cult of fine workmanship, and while remaining faithful to the customs they had brought from Normandy or Brittany, including their patterns, they built up a domestic architecture which gave the countryside of Quebec its special distinction. In the beginning undoubtedly, they had to content themselves with makeshift dwellings made from lumber mixed with field stone, giving little protection against cold, wind or rain. But obstacles were quickly overcome. Very soon there appeared types of Breton houses, short and deep, built in the region of Montreal, or of Norman houses, long and narrow, spread about the neighbourhood of Quebec, both topped with roofs with varying degrees of slope, made of mortar or large stones. The construction of these two types varied according to the imagination of the workmen, the whim of owners, or the exigencies of the climate, without ever losing the trace, for two centuries at least, of their first inspiration which was the classic style of the days of Louis XIV.

Thus the number of parishes increased on both banks of the St. Lawrence, more often within the borders of a seigniory. Together with the missions, they numbered some two hundred in 1760. Parishes and seigniories gave the appearance of a large patriarchal family grouped around the church and presbytery or the humble manor. In these sturdy churches built with taste but without luxury, in these churches with a sloping roof, surmounted by a steeple over the porch on which a weather-vane is installed, the priests and missionaries preached and the flock prayed and sang in French. As the cross had marked the occupation of the land, it continued to mark each step of the prodigious conquest, of the taking root in often ungrateful earth, of men and women who, unknown to themselves perhaps, were also witnesses. Among the settlers, there were some who abandoned agriculture to traffic in furs. They turned *coureurs de bois* through ambition or necessity. Adventurers or not, they played an important part in the voyages of discovery, as indispensible guides and as interpreters among the Indian tribes. On the other hand, they helped to accentuate the dispersal of physical resources, and to slow down the real conquest of the land through agriculture.

Whether settlers or *coureurs de bois*, craftsmen or soldiers, seigniors or officers, the ancestors of modern Canadians were simply men with all of man's qualities and faults. But in spite of the weaknesses inherent in their nature they offered the spectacle, rare enough even at that time, of a people who tried as far as possible to regulate its public and private life in accordance with its principles. Together with their religion, the language — so expressive and authentically French — formed the richest part of their French heritage. Yet other elements of the same heritage had no less value in the eyes of Canadians; a whole body of customs and traditions which ran all the way from laws, beginning with the *Coutume de Paris*, down to popular songs. It was especially through these songs that the purest of French wit was displayed. This French wit was perpetuated by the voices of the men and women who, by the side of the cradle, at the edge of a wood, in the current of a stream, or on the warpath revived the old choruses of love or war. The most astounding fact is not that French culture exercised little influence on letters, arts and sciences at a time when the mother country was indulging in great names and immortal works; what is astounding is that this culture made its way to Quebec and Montreal in spite of obstacles of every nature and kind, and that it took root there sufficiently in order to survive, while waiting to expand far beyond the country of Quebec.

Some sixty years after the founding of Quebec, the greatest of the intendants of New France, Jean Talon, a disciple of Colbert, acknowledged that the little town "could not be better situated should she one day become the capital of a great Empire". At that time, the banks of the St. Lawrence were not slumbering in the silence of the woods : here and there a low house, with sloping roof, framed in the small clearing that marked the first victory of man over the forest or a piled fort guarding the crossing of the river. Then, too, there was *Trois-Rivières*, and especially there was *Ville-Marie*, on the Island of Montreal, fortress and sanctuary which had been born of the dream of a few mystics. As yet these settlements were only like marker's posts upon a trail which was to broaden and lengthen, whose point of departure was known and whose boundary was to be pushed back continuously under the impact of the greed for wealth or the thirst for martyrdom. These posts would never be wrenched from the soil into which they had been driven.

CANADIAN EPIC

In fact, it was between two solid ranks of enemies that some of the best of France's sons were to advance down the long and painful road; sometimes with sword in hand, sometimes with cross, but always bearing with them the vision of the most humane of all countries. When they were not fighting off attacks of the Indians — most often the fierce Iroquois whose boldness knew no limits — it was the English, from London or from Boston, hurling their forces against Acadia or Quebec, appearing suddenly from south or north, always masters of the sea, who had to be fought as far away as Newfoundland, again on the remote frozen wastes of Hudson Bay. New France was embarking upon a century and a half of wars in which the number of victories would be greater than the defeats, and of which the last battle itself would be a victory, but a victory powerless to save an Empire whose destiny was being decided on the plains of Germany.

The achievements were already considerable when Colbert endowed the colony with a Sovereign Council (1663), modelled on that of several provinces in the Kingdom of France, but they were to be even greater fifty or a hundred years later. Resources and means, however, did not keep step with achievement and the day was to arrive, though delayed as long as was humanly possible, when the defences crumbled on all sides, the thin curtain was torn down, and a handful of exhausted warriors was handed over to a stubborn enemy.

Yet the day had not arrived. In this second half of the seventeenth century, which reflected all the splendour of the Sun King at his zenith, the American province received its share of light and warmth, and in turn it had the opportunity to contribute its share of the glory of the mother-country. While the colonist was painfully clearing the lands on both banks of the St. Lawrence and Richelieu rivers, while the soldier, from his wooden forts or from the rock of Quebec, was throwing back the assaults first of the Iroquois tribes, then of the Bostonians and the British sailors, while the very women carried rifles or held the handles of the plough, other men, dreaming again the dream of Cartier or Champlain were determined to pierce the mystery of the lands to the west. Missionaries, traders, *coureurs de bois*, or explorers, moved by the desire to win souls for God, driven by the lure of material gain, or perhaps urged on by a mixture of both motives, plunged into the unknown, never for a moment realizing that even if they did not attain to their set objective, they would yet build an Empire. "Adventurers on the warpath", as Talon described them, they fared forth "to discover unknown countries and to seek for those things which might serve the State". With paddle or oar in hand, a French song on their lips, they feared neither the arrows of the hidden Indian, the biting cold, nor painful hunger. They accepted the long marches through the forest, the weary portages which had to be made around the rapids, nights spent in the open, snow, mud, and the cold north wing; they even accepted death which often came with violence and suffering.

These men were Etienne Brulé, first emissary to Champlain, Jean Nicolet, the discoverer of Lake Michigan, Dollier de Casson and Bréhand de Galinée, Sulpician Fathers, Marquette, a Jesuit, who together with Joliet discovered the Mississipi, Robert Cavelier de La Salle, chief in a gold-embroidered red cloak, and an adventurer with genius, who founded Louisiana, the La Vérendryes, father and sons, who reached the Rocky Mountains. Just as Bienville, Du Lhut, Lamotte-Cadillac, Saint-Lusson and Tonti did, they built forts and founded missions; forts which were only warehouses or trading posts, missions which were always places of refuge. There were others such as Marie de l'Incarnation, Jeanne Mance, Marguerite Bourgeoys, who were foundresses of monasteries, hospitals or schools, François de Montmorency-Laval, first Bishop of Quebec, whose diocese extended from Hudson Bay to the Gulf of Mexico, and many more who were martyrs, namely : Jogues, Daniel, Garnier, Lalemant, Brébeuf, Chabanel, Goupil. Whether these men were Jesuits, Recollets or Sulpicians, they devoted themselves to missionary work in Canada, which is, according to Saint

Vincent of Paul, one of the greatest undertakings of the past fifteen centuries.

Meanwhile, facing each other at daggers drawn in Europe and on the sea, France and Great Britain were fighting with equal ferocity on American soil where they were disputing the empire of the New World and the traffic of furs. The French fought and held out one against five, and soon one against ten or fifteen. At Hudson Bay, Newfoundland and the Antilles, Le Moyne d'Iberville and his brothers victoriously advanced the lilies of France. There were also several incursions in New England and the assault, on two occasions, by the Anglo-American forces which were thrown back from the rock of Quebec. In 1713, the French Empire paid the expenses of the Spanish Succession War. From Hudson Bay to Florida the facade of North America was henceforth English. As masters of Acadia, with the exception of *Ile Royale*, the English commanded the entrance to the St. Lawrence, from the island of Newfoundland. Therefore, they had the monopoly of fishing; they had too the monopoly of the beaver trade, for Hudson Bay was returned to them. How much longer could New France exist, thus encircled?

For the time being at least, France in Europe was intact, and if it had so wished and had taken the proper steps, its colony in America might yet have been saved. But France did not will it, and Canada had few friends in France. It was said that Canada cost too much and brought nothing in return; which was false. With very little help it had succeeded in becoming populated and in providing almost single-handed for its economic life, and now Versailles seemed inclined to saddle the country with the greater part of the burden of its military defense.

In great measure Canada had to fall back on itself. Resuming the economic programme of Talon, the country began to develop its principal resources. With its geographic boundaries henceforth fixed, Canada offered no ground for wild dreams and speculations, contrary to Louisiana. Its government, both military and civil, in principle caused it to be on a same footing as the other provinces of the Kingdom. In practice, a fatherly note characterized the regime. The administrative machine was uncomplicated though red tape was often the cause of frequent and deplorable delays. Save during the last years of the regime, the civil servants were very honest people who carried out their duties with ardour and competence, sometimes with admirable courage. Justice was neither more severe nor less than in the rest of the civilized world. Sons or grandsons of peasants, they themselves were not peasants in the sense usually given to the word under the royal regime. Settled on the land, paying neither salt tax nor any other kind, hunting and fishing in the most complete liberty, obtaining their bread, meat and fish cheaply, masters of their houses, their harvests, and their herds, whether they were peasants or not they preferred to call themselves *habitants*. The word, which served first to distinguish residents from those Frenchmen, whose stay in Canada was only temporary, even if it did not include all those who had become accustomed to Canada, was quickly reserved, as it is today, for the country people, for farmers living on the lands they work.

In town as well as in the countryside, society was not inferior to that elsewhere. There was no marked difference in classes. Undoubtedly there were in Canada, as elsewhere at that time, seigniors and governmental officials, gentlemen, craftsmen and farmers. A social order existed, but such order was not based on money or on nobility. The variety of conditions quickly gave place to a genuine equality, as a result of the equality of risks, sacrifices and trials. Like the priest's house, the seignior's manor was open at all hours. Both curate and seignior were generally pleased to be counsellors, friends and even companions.

The founders quickly gave up the idea of making Frenchmen out of the Indians; but the habitants of New France — city dwellers more so than countrymen — had the means to acquire knowledge. Primary education was free and instruction was given in small schools which were conducted by priests or nuns, who were assisted at times by laymen. In 1635 Quebec was still only a small village when the Jesuits founded there, one year before Harvard, a college for classical education. Twenty-eight years later Mgr. de Laval laid the foundations for the seminary from which, in the middle of the nineteenth century, the university bearing his name was to emerge. Here and there appeared a latin school for boys and a boarding — or day-school for girls.

About the time that the fate of the colony, which, in theory, had been settled by the philosophers, was about to be decided in fact on the sea and on the battlefields of Europe, the face of Canada no longer reflected merely that of France, its mother. In its economic and social life, if not in its laws and institutions, by what intellectual life it possessed, as a vigorous native art was already proving, Canada had not become just another France. Even though it did so unconsciously, it gave sure signs of a personality in which there undoubtedly persisted the traces of its origin, but a personality which stood out sharply from that of other provinces. Canada compared favourably with any of the Provinces of France. There was something feudal about its society, though even that was of a sort peculiar to the country. By reason of the surroundings in which it was born and grew, of the material and spiritual conditions which were not those of France, Canadian society differed appreciably from French society, though from the latter it drew certain features. These it was destined to preserve, for the French Revolution occurred far from the colony and did not touch it. By the time of the Revolution the rupture between the two societies was to be complete. In the meantime the men and women who made up that society had come to America and remained there because they desired to do so. They defended fiercely the new country which they had created somewhat in their own image and which, in its own image, had in one's turn marked them. It is for that reason that from the depths of their hearts there sprung a patriotism which, after the conquest, was to nourish their will to survive.

There was "no rest to be hoped for as long as the French were masters of Canada"; such was the saying in London, as well as in New York and Boston. Finally the hour had come for the British to break the chain of forts which prevented their colonies from spreading out towards the west. The chain was a fragile one and some of its links were missing. Fragile too, was the defence of Canada which had become the pet aversion of the philosophers. It is not astonishing that it was difficult to raise money, command sacrifice, or persuade Versailles to defray urgent expenses.

What is astonishing is that New France resisted, and did so in spite of bad crops and scarcity of provisions, of the lies of conscienceless government officials, of rivalries between leaders, and between subordinates. After each victory it was necessary to retreat, and the outposts fell one after another. On the Plains of Abraham, on the 13th of September, 1759, fifteen minutes were all that were needed by the soldiers of Wolfe, to drive in disorder into a half destroyed Quebec the French troops who bore with them the body of the dying Montcalm. Three days later, the city surrendered. One year later it was the capitulation of Montreal, which Lévis' last victory at St. Foye could not prevent. All this continent of America that France discovered, explored, cleared, and watered with the blood of the best of her sons, was lost forever, as if it were to prove Richelieu right when he said : "The French have more heart to make conquests than head to keep them".

ENGLISH CANADA

So France had lost America. What was to become of the 65 or 70,000 *Canadiens* whose call for help France had not heard ? The conqueror, of course, had formally promised that no French habitant would be deported, that no one would be deprived of his chattles or his land, except religious orders whose fate would be settled when the peace treaty was signed. But what was to become of the language, religion, and laws of the *Canadiens*?

In reality, the question of the use of the French language played no part in the capitulation of Quebec and of Montreal. According to the principles of the law of nations, as well as of English common law, a nation conquered in battle was deprived of none of the distinctive attributes of its nationality, and foremost amongst these was its language. With regard to religion, even though the *Canadiens* had a written guarantee of their right to practise freely their religion, it did not imply that they could practice Roman Catholicism under the authority of the Pope and the bishops, as formerly they had done. As to the customs and laws, the question was settled by the fact that they became "subjects of the King". Words pregnant with meaning, which forecast radical changes in familiar social and political institutions.

Indeed the English proceded without haste and with certain diplomacy during the three years prior to the Treaty of Paris (1763), under a regime which was called the military government, because of the judges who were almost all officers, and the martial law which was applied throughout the country. It was, rather, a severe and hateful form of government, as all occupation regimes use to be, it was a provisional one whose harshness both sides succeeded admirably in mitigating, the victors because they were not devoid of generosity, and the vanquished who were unconscious collaborators. The new masters at London and Quebec, believed perhaps that fine words and charitable deeds were sufficient to lull any mistrust on the part of the *Canadiens*, and prevent any resistance to attempts at assimilation more or less openly confessed. But resignation in no way implied acceptance. Resigned the *Canadiens* certainly were, but they were seriously disturbed at the thought of the fate that might well be theirs, once the war had officially ended.

The *Canadiens* who unwillingly accepted a new allegiance had no occasion to regret the loss of political institutions which they had never known. Accustomed to a regime of absolute authority, on changing allegiance they merely changed masters. Nevertheless the new master spoke a different language, used other laws, and not only professed a different faith, but considered Roman Catholicism as a tissue of lies. In due time, and as soon as they had become used to them, the *Canadiens* would be willing to adopt political institutions to which they were unaccustomed; but they had not the least intention of renouncing their faith, their language, or their laws. They did not believe, and never would believe, that respect for established authority should prevent them from being faithful to their origins. They were firmly resolved to lose nothing of the culture they had made their own, and strengthened the will to survive which had inspired them in the presence of the conqueror.

Fortunately, the *Canadiens*, without political or religious leaders, clinging to their plots of land and grouped around their priests, were not alone in protesting the conditions of the Royal Proclamation issued by George III, a few weeks following the Treaty of Paris. First of all there was Governor Murray, who admired and respected them, and whose indignation was aroused at the attitude of some of his compatriots; in England, too, there were many to condemn the arbitrary action of the King, which favoured the civil laws of the conqueror, and was hostile to the hierarchy of the Catholic Church.

The battle lines were drawn; the struggle was to be lengthy, for it was to endure for almost a century, and on certain issues, it still continues. On the one side was "a handful of ignorant people" who narrowly escaped from material ruin. They had already won the esteem and friendship of a few among the enemies of yesterday, and they would always find some to give proof of such sentiments. Opposed to them, few in number at first, but active, enterprising, self-confident and rich, were the newcomers who monopolized trade, divided the free lands among themselves, bought up seigniories, and established themselves everywhere as masters. Business was their primary interest and they planned to continue and complete, thanks to a Mackenzie, a Thompson and a Fraser, the work of exploration which still proclaimed, and for a long time would continue to proclaim the intrepid courage of the French. Among these there were, and always would be, fanatics, whether traders or officials, for whom everything that was not English and Protestant seemed to have been expressly created and put into this world for the sole end of working for the well-being, the enrichment and the glory of Albion! A minority nevertheless, but an aggressive minority, active and tenacious, which was apt to acquire powerful assistance from both London and Quebec itself, and in a clever way, profit by the errors and weaknesses of the opponent.

Indeed there was quarrelling between two races, and eminent English statesmen unhesitatingly acknowledged the fact, and rallied round as valiant defenders of the *Canadiens*; their energetic mediations, together with the *Canadien's* admirable resistance, gradually obtained justice for the latter, especially through the passing of the Quebec Act (1774). But, racial controversy was not the only bone of contention, since after Canada was divided into two provinces (1791) the struggle was as intense in the one province as in the other : in Upper Canada, whose population was almost entirely English and Protestant, and in Lower Canada, peopled with a French and Catholic majority. At that date, undoubtedly, the official use of the French language had been acknowledged in Lower Canada, as had also the use of French civil law, indeed the only law recognized, and the emancipation of Catholics proclaimed. The consecration of the French fact in America had occurred at the same time as the granting of political liberty to *Canadiens*. When the rudimentary form of government granted in 1774, took on a more normal aspect in 1791, the inhabitants of Lower Canada and those of Upper Canada were called upon to elect their own representatives in the Legislative Assembly, the struggle continued on other grounds, and debates unfolded on a different scene. The *Canadiens* — the term that served to designate for a long time the former subjects of the King of France — were seen to take refuge in a parliamentary system as a means of defence against English intrusion, in order to survive. Moreover, they were the ones, together with a few Englishmen, who demanded the regular and integral functioning of the British parliamentary system. Though London left to the *Canadiens* the free administration of their internal affairs, under the authority of Parliament at Westminster, yet there could not be any question of responsible ministers or control of public funds by the representatives of the people. Powerless therefore to protest against abuses of power on the part of certain governors, or of the Councils, against extortion by certain officials, against the distribution of lands and offices to favourites, the *Canadiens* and their English-speaking allies, in both provinces, eventually found that the measure was full to overflowing. As debate followed debate, voices rose to such a pitch that even the voice of reason was smothered, and in the autumn of 1837, a rebellion broke out.

At the call of Louis Joseph Papineau, an admirer of the Constitution of the United States and a disciple of French liberals, the Patriots took up arms while the Reformers of Upper Canada, headed by William Lyon Mackenzie, rebelled for the same reasons. Sides were not equal. On two occasions, the Patriots and Reformers were outnumbered. Apparently they had failed in their objective. But history today claims that the cause of constitutional government in Canada was won from that moment, and that the two rebellions were the first steps towards autonomy.

But, in the meantime, the English party had triumphed. The dream that some fanatics once had of assimilating, if not destroying, the people conquered in 1763, a dream favoured by many ministers of the Home government but one which Great Britain had appeared to renounce officially, was at last to become a reality. It was unimportant that the Reformers of Upper Canada, English and Protestants, had rebelled; they belonged to the superior race, whereas the Patriots of Lower Canada, without prestige and without leaders, and to quote Alexis de Tocqueville, "remnants of an ancient people adrift on the waves of a new nation", were willed once and for all to disappear. And the means to hasten this inevitable disappearance was there for the taking : the political union of both Canadas.

The men who had conceived and imposed the new regime, in 1840, the authors of a second conquest which was much more dangerous than the military one, could easily push impertinence so far as to deprive the French language of its official characters. A whole system of laws could be imagined to substitute municipal government and school systems, bearing the British trademark, for the parish institutions which, until that time, had been the framework on which French-Canadian social life was built. There were even to be found, among the French Canadians, unconscious allies, who had lost all hope of survival. The hardest and most difficult task still lay ahead.

Two men, with a keen sense of reality, one French-speaking whose name was Louis Hippolyte La Fontaine, the other, English-speaking, Robert Baldwin, understood that a reformed Union, with injustice removed, might work to the advantage of a freer Canada. Once the political question had been settled, the question of nationality would have its turn. And very shortly there came governors with a high conception of their roles as representatives of the British Crown. In London, there were men whom the interests of the Empire, if not sympathy, inclined towards generosity. And especially there were in Canada, Englishmen who understood that without a union of minds, if not a union of hearts, the country could never grow economically or politically.

In less than ten years, the French language had been reestablished and the principle of responsible government was at last acknowledged. Canada was now master, with certain reservations of a secondary importance at that time, of its internal administration. The pressure of events caused it with little delay, to take the first step towards emancipation in the economic field. Though it had already taken a great step forward to political autonomy, and even if through the development of waterways and the construction of railways, its economic life permitted a glimpse of the role that it was destined to play, Canada, with its 2,500,000 inhabitants, had not yet reached the limits of its expansion. To the East and to the West there were other British colonies : the former Acadia, now Nova Scotia, New Brunswick, Prince Edward Island, Newfoundland, the North West Territories, where reigned supreme the Hudson's Bay Company, and, beyond the Rocky Mountains, remote British Columbia. All the colonies, including Canada, had in common only their allegiance to the same Crown and a more or less narrow dependence on a central government : that of London. Intimidated, if not frightened by the young American colossus, they felt the hour was not far distant when a decision, big with consequence, must be taken. Either they must resign themselves to live within borders sharply restricted, and uncertain, or they must further the dream of the founders, and make of it a reality adapted to the needs of the country. That dream was of a nation extending "from ocean to ocean".

Politically separated, the half dozen British colonies of North America were no more closely united in their economic life. This economic life was mostly of an agricultural nature, excepting the fur trade in the North West. The English undoubtedly lost no time in establishing a local industry to meet the needs of the population rather than to compete with that of Great Britain. On the other hand, eighty years after the conquest, United Canada had not moved beyond the stage of first experiments in industry. It did not manufacture for export purposes, though its foreign trade had assumed some importance, From year to year the quantity of furs, lumber and later of wheat, for export to Great Britain, had grown greater, but, as the lands in the West, especially after 1820, had attracted European as well as Canadian immigrants, Canada's principal fear had been that of losing to the United States, the benefits of this trade. There was no doubt that Canada possessed, in the St. Lawrence River, a natural passageway for the entry and dispatch of merchandise. But the St. Lawrence was frozen during the four or five winter months, and in any event men and products from the West had a tendency to reach the American market directly because it was deemed more profitable. It was not easy to resist the attraction of a neighbour that was richer, more thickly populated and better provided with roads, canals and railroads.

If only Canada had known political stability! The governments, which remained a short time in power, sometimes only through the operation of strange combinations, were unable to do any con-

structive work. Both the economic and political unrest were of a
nature to disturb those men who were interested in the future of
Canada, and that of all British possessions. The disquiet was at
its greatest when, in 1860, Civil War broke out in the United States.
Was there not a possibility that Washington might undertake the
conquest of Canada, or at least of those territories still sparsely
inhabited, that stretched from the Great Lakes to the Rockies?
An eventuality all the more plausible since even in London there
were those who advocated that Canada should be abandoned.

Thus it soon became apparent that the only means of escaping
annexation, while at the same time acquiring for the British
Colonies in North America a preferred place in the second British
Empire, was to unite these same colonies by some means or other.
All the colonies desired to pool the various resources whose surplus
would facilitate the expansion of foreign trade, to build a national
industry which would lessen, if not suppress, the state of dependence
towards the American Republic, make of the St. Lawrence the
great commercial artery for the lands of the West, and link the
Atlantic with the Pacific by railroad : but it was useless to dream
of all these things unless the British colonies were united.

When the discussions were begun in earnest in 1865, they lasted
for almost three years, hotly, with animation and at times were
even epic in character. The partisans of the Union were well
aware of the magnitude of their task. There were legitimate
susceptibilities that would have to be carefully spared, reciprocal
concessions that must be made, respect for fundamental rights
that must be assured, and above all, the adherence of French
Canadians had to be obtained; for the latter had no intention of
relinquishing any of their rights which had been acquired at the
cost of a great struggle.

In the end, the ministers at Westminster, who were at first
indifferent, if not actively hostile to the project, announced that
no opposition would be offered to its adoption. On the 29th of
March, 1867, Queen Victoria sanctioned the British North America
Act which was proclaimed on the first day of July of the same year.
Four provinces — to be joined later by six others — had accepted
the necessity of living together under a single government, had
pooled their strength, their resources, their hopes, and also their
debts, in order to assure the progress of each and to maintain the

bonds with Britain. The weakness of spiritual bonds was manifest; the strength of the legal bonds was sufficient, or so it was believed, to compensate for that. As for the French Canadians who were more or less convinced that there could be no hesitation in choosing between a Confederation, in which the rights of minorities would be respected, and annexation to the United States, they entered freely and voluntarily into this Confederation.

A BRITISH DOMINION

On the lst. day of July, 1867, the legislative union between Upper and Lower Canada came to an end. Three British colonies or, more properly speaking, four provinces — Ontario, Quebec, New Brunswick and Nova Scotia — whose combined population exceeded three millions, formed but one state of a somewhat particular type, and was given the name of Dominion of Canada. The Act was more or less clear in defining the powers of a federal government and of each of the provincial governments; but, though the legislative autonomy of these various governments was acknowledged, it granted precedence to the Parliament at London. From a judicial point of view, it is a British Act, though it was the result of an honourable pact between conquerors and conquered of 1760. In fact, there was no longer any question of victors and vanquished. As John Macdonald said, there were only men, equal before the law, citizens of a same country and British subjects who dealt fairly one with the other. For their part, the French Canadians, under the leadership of Georges Etienne Cartier, consented to enter Confederation only with the belief, and on the condition, that their national institutions should be respected everywhere and always, and that their most cherished rights in matters of religion, language, schools and laws should be safeguarded. But, owing to lack of caution, and the great difference which existed between the letter and the spirit of the Act, conflicts would emerge from it which were seriously to compromise the very existence of the Federal form of government, a state of unrest which has not as yet disappeared, especially in the provinces with an English and Protestant majority.

Once the constitution had been adopted, without excessive enthusiasm it is true, but without a resort to force, it remained for the Act to be applied. However, almost two-thirds of British continental possessions in North America remained outside the Dominion. So, the law which had brough about its existence, provided that the union would extend to include these possessions whenever the latter expressed the desire to enter it. Thus, after proceedings more or less difficult, rather violent debates, and incidents at times of a tragic nature : Manitoba, British Columbia, Prince Edward Island, Saskatchewan, Alberta and finally in March 1949, Newfoundland, entered each in turn.

Twenty years had hardly gone by since the birth of the Dominion when a railroad connected — via Montreal — Halifax and Saint John on the Atlantic, with Vancouver on the Pacific. This meant that settlers from Ontario or from other parts of Canada, and thousands of immigrants from both continents would settle the Prairies and make of them the granary of the world. Thanks to the work of construction the very bowels of the earth, as though to justify the explorers of centuries long past, were to reveal riches of nickel and copper, of coal, of lead and zinc, of iron and gold. It was still necessary to populate these territories which were covered with forests and abounded in wild life, and the great prairies where the wild buffalo roamed. Towards the end of the nineteenth century however, in spite of the high birthrate, and the million of immigrants who entered the country, the population of Canada hardly exceeded five million. The lure of the new country — only a halting place for too large a number — had not been as great as the optimists had predicted; certainly not as strong even for the Canadians themselves as the lure of the United States.

Yet considered purely from the point of view of economics, the union of the provinces was not a failure. Agricultural production now not only met all the needs of the local market in full measure, but more and more, from year to year, it contributed to the expansion of Canada's external trade. Even if mining was not proceeding, in 1900, on a scale which it has since reached, it was sufficiently great already to modify sensibly the nature of Canadian trade, of which wheat, the products of the hunt, the fisheries and the forests, still remained the foundation of its trade, but where industrial production was clamouring for a place with great insistɘnce. It was still a new country, and would remain so for a long time to come, whose total external trade had a value of $ 400,000,000 which almost always bought more than it sold, and sold 90 % of its exports to its neighbours or to the London market. Having taken control of its own tariff and customs, Canada did not intend leaving to Great Britain alone the conquering of the markets that might be required.

Canada had set foot in the path of economic prosperity. In a few years it had become a commercial power which could not be ignored. At the same time, but with a somewhat less accelerated pace, the country was setting out upon a political evolution whose final goal was all the more distant and difficult of attainment, in that Canadians themselves were in agreement neither on how to arrive at it, nor on means to speed the journey. Too many powerful interests were involved for Canada to be able to act as a sovereign nation; too often it acted as a colony. There were numerous and narrow bonds which tied Canada to England, namely, judicial, economic or sentimental ones. Undoubtedly, the Governor-General was first and foremost the representative of the Crown; he remained equally the liaison agent between London and Ottawa, as well as the spokesman for ministers in London. In principle, supreme legislative authority still rested with Parliament at Westminster, and the final court of appeal was the Judiciary Committee of the Privy Council in criminal as well as civil cases. While they were no longer regularly imposed, but rather suggested, the wishes of the British government had lost nothing of their strength or influence. Canada was deprived of all sovereignty in international affairs and was not even free to follow the commercial policy best suited to its interests.

Undoubtedly, this vast country had ceased to be merely a geographical expression. But half a century after Confederation, the five million inhabitants of Canada had yet to realize their strength and duty; and an equal feeling of love and respect for their country was yet to be born in their hearts. The unending struggle that the French and Catholic minority was periodically forced to wage in every province, with more or less success, to safeguard or establish its own schools, was sufficient proof.

Leaving out of account the fanaticism and despicable actions of some, and the indifference or maladroitness of others, much ignorance of the facts of history, coupled in many cases with an equal violation of the pledges sanctioned by law, might well have led to the break-up of the union, realized with such difficulty in 1867. Certainly these things did not help to create and disseminate a national spirit which might have served, in place of spiritual bonds, to triumph over political exigencies or economic necessities. They even provoked and nourished among French Canadians, a spirit of nationalism which, in the days of Honoré Mercier, was claimed to owe nothing to politics and gave rise to a struggle which has not as yet been renounced, but is waged whenever necessary, for the rights of minorities and the autonomy of the provinces. It was in the name of this same spirit of nationalism that a grandson of Papineau, the great *patriote* of 1837, Henri Bourassa, undertook to convince Canadians, all Canadians, without distinction of origin, language or religious beliefs, that the time had come for them to take their destiny into their own hands.

One of Canada's greatest statesmen, Sir Wilfrid Laurier, one day prophesized as follows : "The nineteenth century has been that of the United States; the twentieth shall be Canada's century". Very few were those who realized the force of this prophesy in the prosperous year of 1900.

Canada's exports included lumber, fish, cheese, wheat, meat and pelts. It had some coal, but this was found in deposits far distant from the centres where it was most needed; so Canada was forced to import coal from Cumberland or Pennsylvania, and depended on foreign production for the iron ore that its infant industry required. This industry could not expand without the influx of capital from London, New York or Brussels, and sometimes from Paris. Canada has vast water power, but its importance was only beginning to be realized. It leaned, through necessity, towards a moderate form of protection, which left the door open to reciprocity of concessions with the United States, and to preferential duties with Britain and the rest of the Empire. It was a policy of compromise between the free trade tendencies of the western agricultural provinces, and the protectionist leanings of the central provinces, which more and more, particularly Ontario, were becoming heavily industrialized. The export trade was then for Canada, as it is today, a necessity and the sole means of raising the standard of living of its people. The latter had, for the most part, simple tastes. They consumed the products they raised themselves, did without vegetables in winter and tropical fruits all the year round; but they bought dried fruits , sugar and spices, and they drank beer, wine and tea. The art of weaving had not yet completely disappeared; it was still to be found in country districts; but the textile industry was making great strides, and bales of cotton or wool were being imported.

London was forced to submit to the evidence that its American Dominion was less and less resigned to live under a guardianship, even though the guardian, when need arose, was skilled in discretion. Canada must be retained within the framework of the imperial community, and to this end, concessions must be multiplied. Thus, the Parliament at Westminster refrained from exercising its right of veto regarding Canadian legislation. In reality the only Privy Council for the King in Canada was the Federal cabinet. By 1902, not a single British soldier remained in the country and three years later, the command of the Canadian Militia was once and for all given to a Canadian, and British naval bases, in Canadian territory, were transferred to local authorities. The federal government, one day, even announced that unless it were a party to them, Canada would no longer be bound by commercial treaties negotiated in its name by England. The exponents of colonial dependence, however, still had plenty with which to console themselves. The imperial anthem remained the national anthem, the flag was still the Union Jack, and the Canadian was first, if not solely, a British subject. But there was in particular the part that Canada was to play in wars involving the Empire.

If the mother country had thus far persisted in keeping her colonies, even those which had become Dominions, far removed from the hurly-burly of international politics, it had, on the other hand, asked nothing by way of men and money to undertake new conquests, repulse attacks, or launch offensives. At most it had been suggested, without too great insistence, that each colony should be in a position to contribute as much as possible to the defence of its own territory. In that event they had the assurance that the soldiers and sailors of His Britannic Majesty would not leave them to fight alone. Thus when England, about 1850, decided to free herself of the burden she had assumed for the protection of Canada, no one was either surprised or displeased. Indeed, the Canadian statesmen wished for nothing better, since they had hopes of giving to their country, in matters of military defence, the same autonomy that Canada had acquired in the political sphere. It did not for a moment enter anyone's head that a colony might be obliged to take part in those wars in which Great Britain might chance to be engaged in some corner or other of the globe.

The day was not far distant when, in default of regulations and treaties, the imperial government was to decide to appeal to sentiment in an effort to convince the Dominions that they had nothing to lose by becoming active partners of the mother country in an imperial federation directed by London. A first occasion arose, in 1884, when England undertook to conquer the Sudan, and then fifteen years later at the time of the Transvaal war. Though ready to do its share for the defence of its own territory, or indeed for the defence of Great Britain and the Empire, Canada was not inclined to run the risks of an imperial policy which in no way concerned it. But the pressure was so great, that finally the Canadian government agreed to participate in the wars of the Empire on a voluntary basis, and to make an equally voluntary contribution to national defence. On her side, Great Britain understood that it was expedient to inform the Dominions of her foreign policy.

TOWARDS INDEPENDENCE

The years which preceded the first World War were, for Canada, years of great prosperity. The increase in population had not been spectacular; not more than two million in thirteen years. Agriculture in all its forms still dominated the economic life, with wheat heading the list in production as well as export. As with wheat, so with cattle. The great grazing lands of the prairies speedily established the fame of Canadian cattle. To the produce of the forest, such as timber and paper, the export trade had added wood pulp and newsprint. The value of mineral production exceeded $ 100,000,000 and the gross value of manufactured products had passed the $ 2,000,000,000 mark. The gold of the Yukon, the lumber, and particularly the pine wood, of British

Columbia, the nickel and silver of Ontario, the asbestos and wood pulp of Quebec, the coal of Nova Scotia, were already contributing almost as much as agriculture to establish on a solid basis the national wealth of the young nation.

The Canadians of 1914 were a happy people. Like their ancestors and predecessors they were still busy clearing the forest, exploring the underground and building a civilization which did not disregard the spiritual. Few indeed, were the Canadians whose economic or political frontiers extended much beyond the boundaries of their own great country with its vague outlines, of their own province, or indeed of their own community. That peace might be bought at the cost of effort and sacrifices, if not of blood, just as might the patch of ground, the clearing in the forest, the bale of furs, or the ingot of gold, no one could believe for a single moment, not the fisherman of the Maritimes, nor the pioneer settler of the land of Maria Chapdelaine, nor the factory worker in Montreal or Toronto, the cowboy of the Far West, nor the miner of British Columbia.

Nevertheless, it was the war that brought to Canada which neither wished nor sought war, which had no chance to adjudge the question of the origins of the conflict, or in what way it should participate in it, the opportunity to make the most of its immense wealth, and to flood the world with the surplus of its great natural resources. From the very first days it became obvious that Canada's war effort would essentially be an economic one.

However, at that time, Canada had neither a navy nor an army. Yet it managed to raise 600,000 men of which number a great many covered themselves with glory in Flanders and on the Somme; 60,000 of whom did not come back. Yet, Canada's sailors and ships were assuring the protection of the North Atlantic route, and one third of the pilots of the Royal Air Force were Canadians. But Canada which had grown greater in its time of testing, was especially requested to double the extent of its cultivated lands, triple its agricultural production, and increase fourfold its industrial output. Such an effort of production in every aspect of the economic life together with an equally widespread financial effort, had resulted, first of all, in revealing to the world a new Canada unknown even to itself, a Canada far different from the picture carried away by tourists who traversed it in too great a hurry. It was neither another England nor another France, nor was it an imperfect copy or simply an extension of the United States.

The tragic adventure of the war had been turned to its profit. During the conflict, Canada had attained to the full knowledge of its own stature. It had entered upon the war as a colony, submissive to the orders or wishes of the mother country; it had emerged — and Prime Minister, Sir Robert Borden, kept repeating it — as a full partner, or independent State. It was a British nation, certainly, and on more than one account, yet it was equally conscious of the fact that it was as much, if not first and foremost, an American nation. It was called upon, by the nature and wealth of its economy, to take a leading place among the great trading nations, as it was called upon, by its geographic position and its double culture, to serve as a national interpreter between the old and the new world.

Having signed the Treaty of Versailles and having been admitted as a member of the League of Nations, Canada had no intention of stopping suddenly in full course. To be both British and themselves, that was the problem that the Canadians were endeavouring to solve. Meanwhile they were desirous of securing a greater freedom of action in external affairs, and acquiring a more distinctive international personality. This objective was difficult to attain if Canada were not to have diplomatic representation in foreign countries and if it were not free to negotiate political and commercial treaties for itself. From 1921 to 1931, the evolution was completed and the world witnessed the rapid transformation of the British Empire into a Commonwealth or Community of nations. With the Statute of Westminster, and in the following years, traces of colonial dependency gradually disappeared, an evanescence which was marked by the consolidation of the international status of the Dominions, and by absolute recognition of their internal autonomy.

Once the war was over, Canadians had no desire other than to resume the tasks of peace, and to pursue further the experience which they had acquired in industry and in trade. It seemed that Canada's course lay straight before it. It must maintain, or even improve, its advantageous position and continue to exploit its natural resources by the better methods science was placing at its disposal. The automobile, the aeroplane and the radio were instruments designed for a peaceful conquest; hydro-electric power was another. The forest was no longer an obstacle, nor was distance. Great empty spaces to the north, in Quebec, Ontario and Alberta, awaited only the toil of the homesteader to be transformed into agricultural lands, or that of the prospector and miner to surrender their mineral wealth. But the inevitable consequence of this first and rapid change was that Canada was forced to maintain, and even increase, the volume of its exports if it wished to hold its place among the commercial powers and keep up to the standard of living of its people. Would it be possible always to find buyers? That question was most important for Canada; the more important since four-fifths, if not more, of its exchanges were with London and Washington; more with Washington than with London after the war. While trying to solve, as best it could and on the whole wisely, the complex problems of its social life, Canada might never forget that it could have no profitable economic life without heavy exports of its domestic products; the crisis of 1929 was sufficient proof. But, from the testimony of impartial observers, Canada, after four years, was one of the three or four countries which appeared to have embarked on the path of economic recovery, even though unemployment was still at a peak, and though all immigration had been at a standstill. The normal resumption of trade was not, however, possible in a world lulled by illusion, on the edge of an abyss into which it was imperceptibly sliding. With a potential which would have permitted a production capable of satisfying the needs of a population of 75,000,000, and more than ever incapable of living without exporting, Canada needed peace to resume its interrupted climb. Either its great resources, which were still too little appreciated, would continue to contribute to the general prosperity, while serving its own, or the closing of foreign markets would leave the Dominion no alternative but to fit its production to the demands of the national market only. Then perhaps life, which was still not too easy in this new country where so much remained to be done, would resume the gentler rhythm of the pre-war years. Once more, the course of history, almost impossible to foresee and still less to influence for good or evil, was about to turn in Canada's favour.

Until the second Great War, the Dominion retained the conviction that it was isolated geographically and that it had nothing to fear for its security. It thought of itself as a great island protected from any possible attack by three oceans, and the close proximity of the United States, not to mention the British navy. For the French-Canadians, whose attitude ressembled closely that of the great majority of both North and South Americans, Europe was a long way off, and if English-speaking Canadians continued to think of Great Britain first, it was more for sentimental or economic reasons than for military ones. It was therefore difficult, in the years between the two World Wars, to have either group admit that the Western hemisphere's first line of defence was England or the Rhine, and still more difficult to obtain a clear definition of Canada's foreign policy.

Moreover, there could be nothing very distinguished about Canada's foreign policy. It did its best to reconcile its duties as a member of the League of Nations, its tasks as a British country and the obligations imposed upon it by its proximity to the United States. It was essentially from these three sources that were derived the external problems to which the Canadian statesmen addressed themselves more or less willingly until events in Europe awoke, if one might say so, the conscience of the Dominion.

On several occasions, whether it was concerning China, Ethiopia, Austria or Czecho-Slovakia, the liberal Prime Minister, Mackenzie King, a grandson of the "rebel" leader of 1837, said that Canada's decision to participate in a war would be taken only by Parliament or by the Canadian people, in the light of circumstances. It seemed better to allow events to determine the attitude that the Dominion would take in a general conflict; and even then the final attitude would be decided by two factors : a clearly expressed national opinion and, as always, the proximity of the United States.

National opinion was still far from having all the force that only centuries of a life in common can give. At was however strong enough to force recognition of the fact that first consideration must be given to the interests, both immediate and distant, of Canada, a Canada which harboured no dream of expansion, entertained no desire for revenge, and having at its disposal only limited resources, was for that reason incapable of unlimited efforts. As for the proximity of the United States, that fact demanded more and more a line of conduct which did not render too difficult for Canada its role as a British country.

When, on September 19th., 1939, Canada declared war on Nazi Germany, it was no better prepared than in 1914 to play the part of a belligerent. The effective strength of its armed forces hardly exceeded 10,000 men, its navy was almost non-existent, and its budget for national defence was less than $ 65,000,000.

From the Atlantic to the Pacific, from the Great Lakes to the Arctic Circle, the country was soon one immense factory, together with an enormous plain whose proverbial fertility was not the least hope of the nations engaged in a struggle to the death for human liberty. It was no longer sufficient, as it had been in 1914, to transform a few factories into arsenals; all Canada's peacetime industry was mobilized, an industry which devoured men and wore out machines. The allies demanded not only rifles and bullets, but they called for ships, tanks, trucks, guns of all calibres, explosives and airplanes, and naturally, food and clothing too. On the whole, when Germany fell, the total value of Canada's war production exceeded $ 11,000,000,000, thanks to the work of nearly a million men and women employed in war industries, and of more than one million eight hundred thousand engaged in civilian industries. The financial effort was equally astonishing since it not only permitted Canada to meet its direct expenditures for war, but to extend loans, credits or gifts to allied countries, all of which was done in a greater proportion than the United States. Though the economic and financial effort was admirable and worthy of praise, nevertheless, the effective participation of Canadians in the terrible combats which took place on land, at sea, and in the air, was equally spectacular. Up to September 30th., 1945, Canada, whose population was not greatly in excess of 12,000,000, had mobilized more than a million men and women. Of this million, 300,000 had fought on the battlefields of Europe, from the beaches of Normandy to the plains of Germany, in Italy, in the Balkans, and at Hong Kong; an additional 240,000 served in the air force and 100,000 served in the navy and on all the oceans. Canada, therefore, did its share, its very large share, to liberate Europe from Nazi oppression, with the hope that, this time, the sacrifice freely consented to, would not be useless and that it would not have to be renewed against another sort of oppression which would be still more terrible.

TODAY

Canada, which was a French colony for over two centuries, an English possession for almost one hundred years, and a British Dominion between 1867 and 1931, is today one of some twelve autonomous nations bound together under a symbolic tie of common allegiance to one and the same Crown. In fact, what now remains of the legal and political ties which have bound it to England for such a long time? Precisely this : the Crown, and the title of British subject which now shares place with the title of Canadian citizen. No imperial institution can now legally exercice any control over the former colony; neither the sovereign, unless he acts as the Sovereign of Canada and with the advice of his Canadian Councillors, nor the Parliament at Westminster, nor the Ministers at London. The very word Dominion lost its reason for existing, and the Commonwealth has officially ceased to be British. At Ottawa, the Governor-General is only the representative 'of the Crown, and there is nothing to prevent a Canadian from holding this post, as indeed it so came to pass in February 1951.

Completely master of its internal administration, Canada has the same authority over its foreign policy as any other sovereign State. Through its own parliamentary system, it may adopt the laws deemed expedient, and these laws are applied by Canadian courts without possibility of appeal to an Imperial court; it has no accounting to render to anyone, neither to the restricted society to which it belongs nor to the international world. In both cases, equality of rights, if not of fact, is the rule. That Canada is still under the spell of London, is amply demonstrated by its princely gifts or generous loans to England, and its attitude of complacency towards the other members of the Commonwealth; there is no cause for amazement, since family ties whether of birth or adoption are not easily broken, and the voice of blood, when it is not that of mere interest, is a timely reminder of the great law of solidarity which is so necessary to nations as well as to men.

Were it to break tomorrow the last weak chain which links it still to Great Britain and the Commonwealth nations — and no power could prevent it from doing so — Canada could not, by that act, cease to be an American country whose slender population is out of proportion to its natural wealth and the extent of its territories, whose geographical position, rather than its will or its desire, sets out the line of its conduct. Without a certain counter-attraction from London, what would be the result of the attraction of the United States? In the present state of world affairs, and were there be no Commonwealth, how long could Canada avoid playing the part of a satellite nation, a title some are sometimes inclined to confer upon it?

To maintain a fair balance between London and Washington, that is the delicate and difficult problem which Canada must solve. Thus far, in any case, though at a certain cost, Canada has done well enough to reach a somewhat enviable position among the nations, to appear as the link between Europe and America. It is an arduous role, a heavy task, which Canada might successfully essay only if it retains no illusions in regard to its strength, only if it acts always with prudence and wisdom and never forgets that, if its title as an international power confers upon it certain rights, this title also imposes upon it imperious obligations.

An international Power! That is exactly what has become of these remote regions where both French and English started off in search of a new road to the Indies, who contested the fur trade, and where so many men and women gave up their strength or lives to ensure the conversion of infidels and the triumph of their native land. It has also replaced that wild country, an "endless forest", of which the name alone sufficed, during the seventeenth century, to frighten little children who were not too well-behaved. "Small and insignificant communities", such as they were described by Governor-General Durham, more than a century ago. And for so many, only recently, Canada was the land of Maria Chapdelaine!

In the language of political science, this international power is a composite State which lays claim to both confederation and federation. According to the federal plan the government of the ten provinces, the Yukon and North West Territories, hold their prerogatives from the Constitution of 1867, which conferred upon it supreme authority. The power of making laws for all of Canada is vested in a federal parliament composed of a Senate, whose members are appointed for life, and of whom a fixed number is allotted to each province, and of a House of Commons whose members, elected by universal suffrage, are divided among the provinces in proportion to their population. The latter also have, within limits determined by the Constitution, powers proper to them, even though it becomes more and more difficult to maintain a dividing line betwen provincial autonomy and central authority, whose exigencies increase according to the latter's requirements. The Lieutenant-Governor, who is appointed by the Federal cabinet as representative of the Crown, and the local cabinet wield the executive power : a Legislative Assembly elected by popular vote exercices the legislative power in conjunction with, in the Province of Quebec only, a Legislative Council, whose members are appointed by the Crown for life. The Territories are administered by Ottawa directly, assisted by a Council composed of seven members, and the Yukon by a Legislative Council of three members elected by universal suffrage and a Commissioner appointed by the Federal Executive. Finally the exercise of judicial power is divided between the central government and that of each province; the former having the right to appoint the judges of the superior courts of each province, and that of establishing courts of appeal for the entire country, the latter being free to set up lower courts. All these courts of justice deal in criminal matters throughout Canada according to the English criminal law, and in civil matters according to the English Common Law, but only in the nine English provinces; for the Provinces of Quebec kept its French civil laws derived from the *Coutume de Paris* and codified in 1866.

If the Constitution of 1867 was the result of a political agreement between colonial governments responsible but dependent, from the point of view of the facts and in the minds of its authors, it was also the result of a pact between the English and Protestant majority and the French or Catholic minority. They were men, equal before the law, who had dealt fairly one with the other. That was why they were in perfect accord that the Catholic Church — to which 44 % of all Canadians adhere — as well as all the other Churches, should have the right to administer their affairs and develop as they saw fit. It was also for this reason that the French language was given the same official character as that of the English language insofar as federal competency and that of the Province of Quebec were concerned. Moreover, legislation governing schools fell under the exclusive jurisdiction of the provinces. But it must be admitted that the Province of Quebec only, while proclaiming the principle of confessional schools, had entirely respected the rights of the minorities regarding their language and religious beliefs.

The French Canadian language, at times, has come in for commentary, in terms that were either flattering and extreme, or else offensive and unjust. The *Canadiens* of two or three centuries ago spoke the language of their craft and of the native province. But with the passing of years the patois melted into one another to the extend that they now survive only in a variety of local expressions. The greater majority ended up by speaking a language relatively uniform, with the accents and expressions proper to each province, but with the French spoken in the Ile de France dominant. It was not the French of the elite which was not widely used at that time and which, in any case, was not in common usage, even in France, before the end of the eighteenth century; nor was it, to be frank, classical French in all its purity; neither was it a corrupt French nor a patois. Following the example of all languages which are widely spoken, the language of the *Canadiens* had assumed, and has retained in spite of syntactical errors, incorrect usages, and barbarisms, the character of a regional dialect, in which archaisms abound, and borrowings from foreign languages with which it has been in contact are not infrequent. Though the language has not always, and everywhere, retained its purest form, and that through its accent, as changeable in Canada as well as in France, it may, at times, grate upon or offend a delicate ear, it is neither astonishing nor shocking since it is a language which has been holding its own for almost two centuries.

To sum up, it was not a marriage of love that the Canadians entered into almost one hundred years ago, but one of convenience, and there is nothing to prove that a marriage of convenience should necessarily and always be an unhappy union. Neither is it essential that the *modus vivendi* which flows therefrom be constantly devoid of cordiality. Some 15,000,000 Canadians today are a striking example, despite the darker sides to the picture. The problem is far from being simple. One of the aspects, and not the least, is that which concerns 3,000,000 New Canadians who have come from different parts of Europe and the United States, particularly in the last half-century, to which number are added each year, 150,000 to 200,000 immigrants. But there is another side that is far more serious : the co-existence of two ethnical groups which form the bulk of the population of Canada. Over 6,000,000 Canadians are of British origin and English-speaking; over 4,500,000, of whom one million at least reside outside the Province of Quebec, are of French descent and French-speaking. On one side is the English fact representing the greater in number and material wealth, which one would be stupid to deny, and on the other, the French fact that has been growing stronger for the past three centuries and is continuing to do so, not only in the social, intellectual and political life of Canada, but in that of its economic activity. Too many Anglo-Canadians, on their own admission, obstinately refuse fully to appreciate this French fact. Therefore, in both cases, it is not a question of sacrificing their essential characteristics, but mutually to acknowledge, in words and actions, their equality of rights, without which there can be no equality of sacrifices and duties. Contrary to what has occurred in the American melting-pot, Canada remains, according to the words of its present Prime Minister, The Right Honourable Louis Saint-Laurent, "a nation based on the union of the descendants of two great races, enjoying equal rights".

To these men whose origin, language and religion were different, who became united in order to form a great nation and who earnestly desired happiness and prosperity, Canada today offers them the most precious of advantages. These same advantages are also offered to millions of human beings, whose misery, anxiety, or hope for easier circumstances, inclined them to picture Canada as a sort of Eldorado, Merlin the Magician or a horn of plenty. And yet, a fortune is not gained by the mere fact of setting foot on Canadian soil. Extremes should be avoided if one wishes to be spared deceptions and surprises which may occur in both instances. Neither in Canada nor elsewhere are fortunes made over night, and from this point of view, Canada is not a land of miracles. It is still a young country, and consequently a rugged one, where climatic conditions are rather freakish and very severe at times, with in addition, great distances to cover. One must also take into account the mode of living which is quite different to that of the

Americans, in the narrow sense of the word, and is not altogether that of Europe. Over and above the physical climate, which greatly impressed the Frenchmen of the sixteenth and seventeenth centuries, the moral and intellectual atmosphere is often of a nature to surprise, if not distress new comers, at first blush to say the least.

Canada, we repeat, had not solved all its problems of a national, social or cultural order, set by its vertiginous transformation and the prevailing conditions of a troubled world. But it endeavoured to clarify and ward them off with some success, while being moreover alive to the inevitable results of labour conflicts. It was with giant strides that Canada advanced on the road to economic prosperity. During the past fifteen years, has it not more than doubled its industrial production? Has not the gross value of its national production increased from $ 3,500,000,000 in 1938, to $ 24,000,000,000 in 1954; that of its mining production from $ 475,000,000 to over $ 1,200,000,000; that of its forestry production, including pulp and paper, from $ 158,000,000 to $ 1,500,000,000? Has not its iron and steel production tripled, the fabrication of electrical equipment increased fourfold? And its water power development been carried to the extent of about 15,000,000,000 horse-power? And has not the total value of its foreign trade amounted to $ 8,800,000,000 in 1955? Undoubtedly, over half of this trade (60 %) is carried on with the United States alone. Moreover, Canada exports an enormous quantity of raw materials, primary products, the conversion of which, at home, would prove more advantageous. The exhaustion of all this wealth is to be feared if elementary precautions are not taken, for overproductivity is not a safeguard against unforeseen contingencies. Nevertheless, the Canadian dollar, for the moment, is the firmest and strongest currency in the world — a situation which may not always be convenient. Inflation has not been completely controlled, though it is not felt in Canada as much as elsewhere, in spite of the fact that the State and individuals have a tendency to live beyond their means, as people do everywhere else. Even though agriculture no longer represents more than 7 % of the national wealth, agricultural production, notwithstanding a decrease in rural labour, is always considerable; wheat yielded 513 million bushels in 1954.

The cost of living is certainly high in Canada. Imposts are

heavy in order to meet the requirements of national defence, at a cost of $ 5,000,000,000 in three years (1951-53), and to assume the overwhelming burden of social security. The increase in the adverse trade balance is another cause of anxiety, and more so the state of economic dependency in which Canada is placed regarding its foreign trade, especially with the United States from whence comes most of its imports (65 %) and the highest percentage of capital ($ 9,000,000,000 in 1955) necessary to the expanding of its industries or the development of its natural resources. Yet, who can prophesy the limit of Canada's resources, granting that there is one? At present, Canada leads in the production of nickel, cobalt, asbestos and newsprint, ranks second in the production of gold and zinc, third in copper, and fourth in silver and lead. It ranks with the Belgian Congo as the country richest in uranium deposits, and is the Commonwealth's principal producer of petrol with 90 million barrels to its credit in 1955. Alberta has immense reserves of petrol which have only recently been discovered, yet this petrol is already being transported by pipeline from Edmonton to Sarnia (Ontario), that is to say, a distance of 1,765 miles. Another pipeline heads through the Rockies, from Edmonton to Vancouver, on the Pacific (718 miles). Alberta also produces gas which will be conveyed by means of pipeline as far as Montreal, a distance of 2,570 miles. And have not zinc and copper deposits been discovered in Quebec as well as copper and nickel in Manitoba? And what of the iron deposits in Ungava (New Quebec) or Labrador, the development of which has just started (1954) following the building of railroads and plants at a cost of $ 300,000,000? Then, in order to facilitate the transportation of these millions of tons of ore titanium to plants in the western and central parts of the United States, Canada has decided to undertake, with the cooperation of its neighbour for their own part, the canalization of the St. Lawrence River above Montreal, even if the project should cost itself $ 300,000,000 or more.

Though in the Province of Quebec, Canada has the largest aluminium refinery in the world, another as large, if not still larger, is already in operation in British Columbia. In the latter Province, as well as in Alberta and Quebec, new hydro-electric plants are unceasingly contributing towards increasing the production of water power, which has already caused Canada to rank immediately after the United States in this respect. As these plants are erected in remote centres in the north of those provinces, if not in the Great Canadian North, additional railroads are built through rock or forest, over and above the 43,500 miles which Canada already has. But wherever possible the highway supplements or procedes the rail. Thus, Canada at present has 437,500 miles of highways, of which about 180,000 are coated with asphalt or gravel, including the Alaska Highway, open all year round, and which extends 1,250 miles in the national territory, to which it is planned to add a railroad; and this without including the Trans-Canada highway, which will measure more than 5,000 miles when completed.

Still it must not be forgotten that where roads and railways are out of the question, the rivers and lakes may always be used for transportation purposes. There are also the airlines which Canadians are resorting to as a means of travelling from one ocean to another, from province to province and from one city to another; from French Quebec to Ottawa, the federal capital, to Winnipeg, Regina or Edmonton, prairie cities which have grown overnight, like mushrooms; from Halifax, on the Atlantic, to Montreal, the cosmopolitan Metropolis, mostly French; from Toronto, the Queen City, to Vancouver, gateway to the Orient. Winter and summer, people travel back and forth, especially between the months of April and November; whether they travel on business or for pleasure, they delight in the soft landscapes of Nova Scotia and seek the splendours of the mountainous seaboard of Gaspesia, the peaceful lakes of Quebec and Ontario, abounding in fish, or the magnificent scenery of the Rockies or the impressive Pacific Coast. Let it be repeated that except in southern British Columbia, Canadian winters are long and severe, although there are days which are surprisingly clear and favourable to sports; spring bursts forth radiantly and abruptly with buds and sap which closely follow on the breaking-up of the ice on lakes and rivers; summer lasts about two or three months, and autumn is the most dazzling season when the forests, transformed into parks or not, offer a feast to the eye, the gamut of tones of green, yellow and red.

Undeniably, |Canada has become a great economic power whose wealth is a source of envy and hope to millions of human beings, a nation that is master of its political destiny, insofar as independence and freedom do ever exist for nations and individuals, a country whose religious and social institutions ensure stability insofar as this is possible in a troubled and changing world. But a nation is never truly great unless it be sustained by mental culture, the radiance of which extends beyond its boundaries, and if besides priding itself on its economic activity, it takes the same pride in its writers, artists and scientists. Now, in Canada, it has so happened that progress on the material plane, while not diverting attention from mental culture, has occurred at a faster rhythm than advancement in letters, arts and sciences. Undoubtedly, Canada is not lacking in schools, colleges or universities, and its school population numbers 2,400,000 students, if not more, including both sexes. No doubt also, scientific research is gaining more and more fame, judging by the work carried out by Canadian scientists, in radar, atomic energy and nuclear physics, not to mention surgery of the heart and that of the nervous system. It would especially be unfair to underestimate the valuable contribution mankind owes to the Canadian nation for the genius it has displayed in its drive towards material progress, in spite of the fact that it still remains for this nation to endeavour to provide the same amount of energy and steadfastness in the service of intellectual values.

Does this imply that the Canadian nation is entirely devoid of culture? It would be very stupid to presume so, for if Canada cannot lay claim to a real national culture, nevertheless, it possesses all the elements of producing one, the day that both English and French cultures shall unite, without merging. These two cultures which attest to the double ethnical origin of the greater part of the population, are indeed, a wonderful asset to the country. But, from a cultural point of view as well as that of national affairs, the same problem creates the same distinction, a problem all the more difficult to solve owing to the duality of languages and of intellectual formation.

Canada, a fountain of civilizing ideas in a tormented world, appears to be a country of two cultures : that of French-speaking Canadians, which was acquired, as far as possible, from Latin and French sources; and that of English-speaking Canadians, which must not be confused with American culture, and which is indebted to Europe in great part. Once again, economic maturity came to Canada at the same time as that of political maturity, when not slightly preceded by it. Intellectual maturity is still to come, though brilliant demonstrations have already marked its prelude, even though the master-work which would have the agreement and consent of all, is yet to arrive.

It is an acknowledged fact that a distinctively Canadian art, descended in a direct line from the purest tradition of French provinces, itself inspired by the classical tradition of the Great Century, existed prior to 1760 and resisted for some time the effects of the conquest. This style was especially manifest in religious or domestic architecture, ornamental sculpture and the craft of the goldsmith. Then came academism in all its forms, which resulted, chiefly in ensuring easy fortunes to the spoilers of plaster, and the champions of false Roman and false Gothic styles. A few structures erected after 1920 that are worthy of attention and inspire respect, are the great grain elevators of Port Arthur or Montreal, and the new university of the latter city. These structures evidence boldness of concept without, however, giving to Canadian architecture the radiance to which it has a right to aspire.

It is not altogether the same with sculpture, where the vice of traditionalistic forms had just begun to loosen its grip towards 1920, and in which examples of statuary monuments, rustic carving and religious art show no disdain of daring modernism. It is in the field of painting that evolution or revolution has been more pronounced, the demonstration of a new life is more marked. A true Canadian school of painting would be sought in vain. On the other hand, it is certain that the art of Canadian painters has, for the past century and a half, developed beyond the stage of groping, and that particularly during the last twenty-five years, it has become humane, universal, unquestionably animated, abounding in strength and boldness.

What is true of painting is equally true of music; a truly Canadian music has not yet put in an appearance. Music, in Canada, has as yet taken on no national character. Canadian composers still express themselves, a little too timidly in the musical language of the countries of their origin, so much so that music in Canada is either partly English or partly French. If to this is added the remarkable forward drive given to the study of music during the past twenty-five years, the performance of symphony orchestras which has practically attained perfection, the brilliant success of artists who are increasing in number, and are eagerly sought after, it is evident that musical civilization in Canada has ceased to be a promise and has become a reality.

The existence of a Canadian literature, whether of French or English expression, is no longer in doubt, especially if one admits that poetry, the novel or the theater are not the only elements of literature. The literary production of French Canadians which dates back to a century ago, and that of English Canadians, which is of a more recent dating, have never been so intense. The number of writers and their works, as well as the quality thereof, is sufficient proof. The Canadian intellect has acquired a certain maturity which was unknown at the beginning of the twentieth century. Progress is seen in university study; research in all fields has been carried out with more scientific methods, with the result that the dividing wall which formerly existed between literature and reality has to a great extent disappeared. A more learned public, and also a greater one, has developed a taste for books, and the fame of several Canadian writers has extended beyond the borders. Nevertheless the Canadian writer, whether English — or French — speaking, has not overcome all the obstacles barring his way towards ranking with the best of his time. But Canada does boast of novelists, narrators and historians, poets and critics, even, more recently dramatists who compare favourably with those of other literatures, excepting of course the greatest. Moreover, in the matter of comparisons, must one always seek them in Paris, London or New York?

According to certain indications — among which is the Royal Commission on letters, arts and science (1949-50) — interest in the things of the mind has greatly increased. Many Canadians are now convinced that the time has come, at long last, to make use of their intellectual resources for the enrichment of national life and for the shining forth of that same life by culture, whilst protecting the latter against the dangers of "americanization", the boldness of which is more and more apparent.

Once again, this culture is dual; it is French or English, or French and English. But it would be a mistake to confound it with that of France or England. None other than Mr. Etienne Gilson, of the French Academy, has it seems more clearly settled the question, when he writes: "On the banks of the Saint Lawrence there exists a nation of French Culture; but this nation is not in debted to us for such culture; it flows therethrough like a sap, not ours, but theirs". This testimony is as apt for those of English culture. Moreover, for the one as for the other, the old motto of Quebec has lost none of its profound meaning : *Je me souviens*.

Jean *BRUCHESI.*
of The Royal Society of Canada.

1. BAIE DE PLAISANCE (TERRE-NEUVE).
PLAISANCE BAY (NEWFOUNDLAND).

2. LA PÊCHE AUX CAPELANS (TERRE-NEUVE).
CAPELIN FISHING (NEWFOUNDLAND).

3. USINES DE PATE DE BOIS ET DE PAPIER A JOURNAL (TERRE-NEUVE).
PULPWOOD AND NEWSPRINT PLANTS (NEWFOUNDLAND).

4. LA PÊCHE AU HOMARD (TERRE-NEUVE).
LOBSTER FISHING (NEWFOUNDLAND).

5. LA PÊCHE AU HOMARD (TERRE-NEUVE).
LOBSTER FISHING (NEWFOUNDLAND).

7. CHAMP DE POMMES DE TERRE (ILE DU PRINCE-ÉDOUARD).
POTATO FIELD (PRINCE EDWARD ISLAND).

8. UNE PLAGE (ILE DU PRINCE ÉDOUARD).
A BEACH (PRINCE EDWARD ISLAND).

9. DANS L'ILE DU CAP-BRETON (NOUVELLE-ÉCOSSE).
CAPE BRETON ISLAND (NOVA SCOTIA).

10. HALIFAX (NOUVELLE-ÉCOSSE).
HALIFAX (NOVA SCOTIA).

11. UN VILLAGE SOUS LA NEIGE (NOUVELLE-ÉCOSSE).
SNOWED-IN VILLAGE (NOVA SCOTIA).

12. POMMIERS EN FLEURS.
APPLE TREES IN BLOOM.

13. LES BŒUFS.
A YOKE OF OXEN.

14. LE PUITS D'ÉVANGÉLINE, A GRAND-PRÉ (NOUVELLE-ÉCOSSE).
EVANGELINE'S WELL AT GRAND PRE (NOVA SCOTIA).

15. LABOURAGE D'AUTOMNE (NOUVELLE-ÉCOSSE).
FALL PLOUGHING (NOVA SCOTIA).

16. UNE FERME (NOUVELLE-ÉCOSSE).
A FARM (NOVA SCOTIA).

17. RÉGATES A CHESTER (NOUVELLE-ÉCOSSE).
CHESTER REGATTAS (NOVA SCOTIA).

18. VILLAGE DE PÊCHEURS (NOUVELLE-ÉCOSSE).
A FISHING VILLAGE (NOVA SCOTIA).

19. UN HAVRE DE PÊCHE (NOUVELLE-ÉCOSSE).
A FISHING HAVEN (NOVA SCOTIA).

20. LA PÊCHE A LA TRUITE (NOUVELLE-ÉCOSSE).
TROUT FISHING (NOVA SCOTIA).

21. UN PHARE (NOUVELLE-ÉCOSSE).
A LIGHTHOUSE (NOVA SCOTIA).

22. LA CATHÉDRALE ANGLICANE DE FREDERICTON (NOUVEAU-BRUNSWICK).
THE ANGLICAN CATHEDRAL AT FREDERICTON (NEW BRUNSWICK).

23. LA BÉNÉDICTION DES BARQUES (NOUVEAU-BRUNSWICK).
THE BLESSING OF THE FISHING FLEET (NEW BRUNSWICK).

24. LE PONT DE QUÉBEC (PROVINCE DE QUÉBEC).
THE QUEBEC BRIDGE (PROVINCE OF QUEBEC).

25. LA CHUTE MONTMORENCY (P. DE QUÉBEC).
MONTMORENCY FALLS (P. OF QUEBEC).

26. BASSE VILLE ET PORT DE QUÉBEC (P. DE QUÉBEC).
LOWER TOWN AND QUEBEC HARBOUR (P. OF QUEBEC).

27. LE CHŒUR DE LA BASILIQUE
    NOTRE-DAME (QUÉBEC).
   THE CHANCEL OF THE BASILICA
    OF NOTRE-DAME (P. OF QUEBEC).

28. UN CORRIDOR DU MONASTÈRE
    DES URSULINES (QUÉBEC).
  A CORRIDOR IN THE URSULINE
    MONASTERY (QUEBEC).

29. L'HOTEL CHATEAU FRONTENAC, A QUÉBEC (P. DE QUÉBEC).
THE CHATEAU FRONTENAC HOTEL, AT QUEBEC (P. OF QUEBEC).

30. PLAN DE QUÉBEC EN 1809 (P. DE QUÉBEC).
PLAN OF THE CITY OF QUEBEC, IN 1809 (P. OF QUEBEC).

31. LA CITADELLE DE QUÉBEC (P. DE QUÉBEC).
THE CITADEL OF QUEBEC (P. OF QUEBEC).

32. RUE DES GLACIS, A QUÉBEC (P. DE QUÉBEC).
DES GLACIS STREET, AT QUEBEC (P. OF QUEBEC).

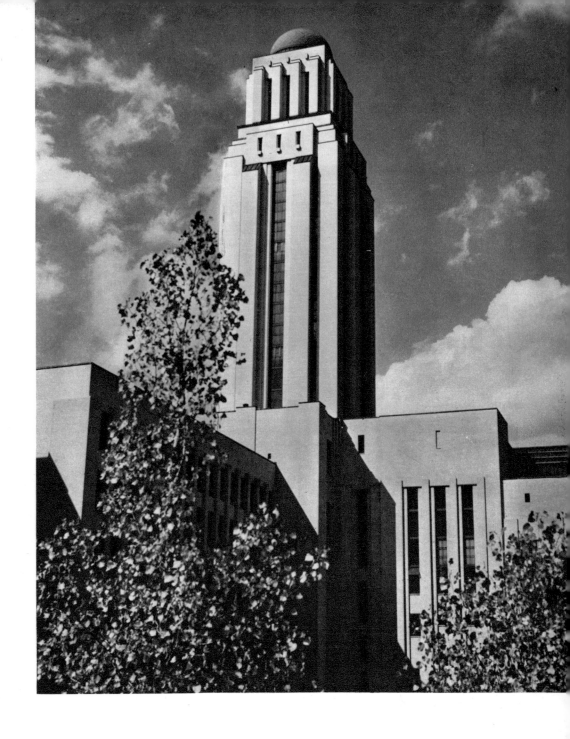

33. LA TOUR DE L'UNIVERSITÉ DE MONTRÉAL (P. DE QUÉBEC).
THE TOWER OF THE UNIVERSITY OF MONTREAL (P. OF QUEBEC).

34. MONTRÉAL (P. DE QUÉBEC).
MONTREAL (P. OF QUEBEC).

35. MONTRÉAL VERS 1800 (P. DE QUÉBEC).
MONTREAL TOWARDS 1800 (P. OF QUEBEC).

36. LES TOURS DE LA MONTAGNE, MONTRÉAL (P. DE QUÉBEC).
THE TOWERS OF THE MOUNTAIN, MONTREAL (P. OF QUEBEC).

37. ORATOIRE SAINT-JOSEPH, MONTRÉAL (P. DE QUÉBEC).
SAINT JOSEPH'S ORATORY, MONTREAL (P. OF QUEBEC).

38. ÉGLISE NOTRE-DAME, MONTRÉAL (P. DE QUÉBEC).
THE CHURCH OF NOTRE-DAME, MONTREAL (P. OF QUEBEC).

39. CHATEAU DE RAMEZAY, A MONTRÉAL (P. DE QUÉBEC).
CHATEAU DE RAMEZAY, AT MONTREAL (P. OF QUEBEC).

40. PERCÉ ET SON ROCHER (P. DE QUÉBEC).
PERCÉ AND ITS FAMOUS ROCK (P. OF QUEBEC).

41. L'ILE BONAVENTURE (P. DE QUÉBEC).
BONAVENTURE ISLAND (P. OF QUEBEC).

42. PORT DE PÊCHE GASPÉSIEN (P. DE QUÉBEC).
A FISHING PORT AT GASPÉ (P. OF QUEBEC).

43. BARQUES DE PÊCHE (P. DE QUÉBEC).
FISHING-BOATS (P. OF QUEBEC).

44. MONT SAINT-PIERRE (P. DE QUÉBEC).
MONT SAINT-PIERRE (P. OF QUEBEC).

45. ÉGLISE DE SAINT-PIERRE (ILE D'ORLÉANS, P. DE QUÉBEC).
THE SAINT-PIERRE CHURCH (ISLAND OF ORLEANS, P. OF QUEBEC).

46. UNE ÉGLISE DE CAMPAGNE (P. DE QUÉBEC).
A COUNTRY CHURCH (P. OF QUEBEC).

47. CHAPELLE DE PROCESSION (P. DE QUÉBEC).
A PROCESSION CHAPEL (P. OF QUEBEC).

48. SAINT-JEAN-PORT-JOLI (P. DE QUÉBEC).
SAINT JEAN PORT JOLI (P. OF QUEBEC).

49. LA CAMPAGNE QUÉBÉCOISE (P. DE QUÉBEC).
THE QUEBEC COUNTRYSIDE (P. OF QUEBEC).

51. MAISON DANS LA NEIGE (P. DE QU
A SNOW-BANKED HOUSE (P. OF QU

50. VIEILLE MAISON CANADIENNE (P. DE QUÉBEC).
AN OLD CANADIAN HOUSE (P. OF QUEBEC).

52. VIEILLE MAISON CANADIENNE (P. DE QUÉBEC).
AN OLD CANADIAN HOUSE (P. OF QUEBEC).

53. VIEILLE MAISON CANADIENNE (P. DE QUÉBEC).
AN OLD CANADIAN HOUSE (P. OF QUEBEC).

54. VIEILLE MAISON CANADIENNE (P. DE QUÉBEC).
AN OLD CANADIAN HOUSE (P. OF QUEBEC).

55. VIEILLE MAISON CANADIENNE (P. DE QUÉBEC).
AN OLD CANADIAN HOUSE (P. OF QUEBEC.).

56. MOULIN SEIGNEURIAL AUX ÉBOULEMENTS (P. DE QUÉBEC).
SEIGNORIAL MILL AT LES EBOULEMENTS (P. OF QUEBEC).

57. MOULIN A VENT (P. DE QUÉBEC).
A WIND MILL (P. OF QUEBEC).

58. LES TROIS MARIE AU TOMBEAU LE MATIN DE PAQUES.
THE THREE MARYS AT THE TOMB ON EASTER MORNING.

59. LE BEAU DIEU.
"LE BEAU DIEU".

60. LA MADONE.
THE MADONA.

61. TABERNACLE EN BOIS SCULPTÉ.
   A TABERNACLE CARVED IN WOOD.

62. INTÉRIEUR D'ÉGLISE.
   THE INTERIOR OF A CHURCH.

63. LE PIN GRIS.
THE JACK PINE.

64. L'ESCLAVE.
THE SLAVE.

65. EX-VOTO.
EX-VOTO.

66. LA CHASSE AUX TOURTRES.
"LA CHASSE AUX TOURTRES" (PASSENGER PIGEONS).

67. NATURE MORTE AUX DOMINOS.
A STILL LIFE "DOMINOS".

68. LA RÉCOLTE DE L'EAU D'ÉRABLE (P. DE QUÉBEC).
THE GATHERING OF MAPLE WATER (P. OF QUEBEC).

ORIGNAL SORTANT DE L'EAU.
A MOOSE COMING OUT OF THE WATER.

70. LA CHASSE A L'ORIGNAL (P. DE QUÉBEC).
MOOSE HUNTING.

71. LA PÊCHE A LA LIGNE.
ROD FISHING.

72. QUAND LA JOURNÉE EST TERMINÉE (P. DE QUÉBEC).
WHEN DAY IS DONE (P. OF QUEBEC).

73. LE MARCHÉ (P. DE QUÉBEC).
THE MARKET PLACE (P. OF QUEBEC).

74. LES FOINS (P. DE QUÉBEC).
HAYING-TIME (P. OF QUEBEC).

75. INTÉRIEUR D'UNE MAISON RURALE (P. DE QUÉBEC).
INTERIOR OF A RURAL HOUSE (P. OF QUEBEC).

76. LABOUR SUR L'ILE D'ORLÉANS (P. DE QUÉBEC).
    PLOUGHING (ISLAND OF ORLEANS, P. OF QUEBEC).

77. LA FOURNÉE (P. DE QUÉBEC).
THE BAKING OF BREAD (P. OF QUEBEC).

78. LE FOUR A PAIN (P. de QUÉBEC).
BREAD OVEN (P. OF QUEBEC).

79. VAL-MORIN (P. DE QUÉBEC).
VAL MORIN (P. OF QUEBEC).

80. UNE CHUTE DANS L'UNGAVA (P. DE QUÉBEC).
A WATER-FALL IN UNGAVA (P. OF QUEBEC).

82. LA "DRAVE".
"LA DRAVE".

FLOTTAGE DU BOIS.
THE FLOATING OF LOGS (P. OF QUEBEC).

83. USINES HYDRO-ÉLECTRIQUES (P. DE QUÉBEC).
HYDRO-ELECTRIC PLANTS (P. OF QUEBEC).

84. EN PLEINS RAPIDES.
IN THE RAPIDS.

85. AMAS DE BILLES DE BOIS POUR LA FABRICATION DU PAPIER.
A PILE OF LOGS.

87. ACIÉRIE.
STEEL-WORKS.

88. MINERAI DE FER.
IRON ORE.

89. LE CURLING.
CURLING.

90. SPORT D'HIVER : LE HOCKEY.
HOCKEY: A WINTER SPORT.

91. OTTAWA (P. D'ONTARIO).
OTTAWA (P. OF ONTARIO).

92. LA TOUR DE LA PAIX, OTTAWA (P. D'ONTA
THE PEACE TOWER, OTTAWA (P. OF ONTA

93. LE FORT HENRY, A KINGSTON (P. D'ONTARIO).
FORT HENRY, AT KINGSTON (P. OF ONTARIO).

94. TORONTO (P. D'ONTARIO).
TORONTO (P. OF ONTARIO).

95. SUR LE LAC CALME (P. D'ONTARIO).
ON A QUIET LAKE (P. OF ONTARIO).

96. LES CHUTES DU NIAGARA (P. D'ONTARIO).
NIAGARA FALLS (P. OF ONTARIO).

97. EN PLEINE FORÊT (P. D'ONTARIO).
DEEP IN THE FOREST (P. OF ONTARIO).

98. LE CANAL WELLAND (P. D'ONTARIO).
WELLAND CANAL (P. OF ONTARIO).

99. FORT-WILLIAM (P. D'ONTARIO).
FORT WILLIAM (P. OF ONTARIO).

100. LES PRAIRIES (P. DU MANITOBA).
THE PRAIRIES (P. OF MANITOBA).

101. UN CHEF SAUTEUX.
A SAUTEUX CHIEF.

103. UNE FERME AU MANITOBA.
A FARM IN MANITOBA.

104. LA CHASSE AUX CANARDS (P. DU MANITOBA).
DUCK-HUNTING (P. OF MANITOBA).

105. LA RIVIÈRE WINNIPEG (P. DU MANITOBA).
THE WINNIPEG RIVER (P. OF MANITOBA).

108. LA MOISSON (P. D'ALBERTA).
THE HARVEST (P. OF ALBERTA).

109. LA MOISSON (P. D'ALBERTA).
THE HARVEST (P. OF ALBERTA).

110. TRANSPORT PAR EAU (P. D'ALBERTA).
WATER TRANSPORT (P. OF ALBERTA).

111. PUITS D'HUILE (P. D'ALBERTA).
OIL-WELLS (P. OF ALBERTA).

112. LA GRAND'ROUTE CALGARY-BANFF (P. D'ALBERTA).
THE CALGARY-BANFF HIGHWAY (P. OF ALBERTA).

113. LE TRAIN DANS LES ROCHEUSES (P. D'ALBERTA).
A TRAIN IN THE ROCKIES (P. OF ALBERTA).

116. LAC MORAINE (P. D'ALBERTA).
LAKE MORAINE (P. OF ALBERTA).

E GRAND HOTEL DE BANFF (P. D'ALBERTA).
THE GRAND HOTEL AT BANFF (P. OF ALBERTA).

117. LAC MALIGNE (P. D'ALBERTA).
LAKE MALIGNE (P. OF ALBERTA).

118. UN LAC DANS LES ROCHEUSES.
A LAKE IN THE ROCKIES.

119. DANS LES ROCHEUSES (COLOMBIE-BRITANNIQUE).
IN THE ROCKIES (BRITISH COLUMBIA).

120. LA GRANDE DIVISION (P. D'ALBERTA ET DE LA COLOMBIE-BRITANNIQUE).
THE GREAT DIVIDE (P. OF ALBERTA AND BRITISH COLUMBIA).

121. ANSE-A-JERVIS (COLOMBIE-BRITANNIQUE).
JERVIS COVE (BRITISH COLUMBIA).

122. UNE RIVIÈRE (COLOMBIE-BRITANNIQUE).
A RIVER (BRITISH COLUMBIA).

123. TROUPEAU DE MOUTONS (COLOMBIE-BRITANNIQUE).
A FLOCK OF SHEEP (BRITISH COLUMBIA).

124. TOTEMS (COLOMBIE-BRITANNIQUE).
TOTEM POLES (BRITISH COLUMBIA).

125. POMMIERS AU BORD DE LA MER (COLOMBIE-BRITANNIQUE).
AN ORCHARD (BRITISH COLUMBIA).

126. VANCOUVER (COLOMBIE-BRITANNIQUE).
VANCOUVER (BRITISH COLUMBIA).

127. BATEAUX DE PÊCHE (COLOMBIE-BRITANNIQUE).
FISHING-BOATS (BRITISH COLUMBIA).

128. LA PÊCHE AU SAUMON (COLOMBIE-BRITANNIQUE).
SALMON FISHING (BRITISH COLUMBIA).

129. VICTORIA (COLOMBIE-BRITANNIQUE).
VICTORIA (BRITISH COLUMBIA).

130. UNE PLAGE SUR LE PACIFIQUE (COLOMBIE-BRITANNIQUE).
A BEACH (BRITISH COLUMBIA).

131. EN AVION.
FLYING.

COMMENTS
ON ILLUSTRATIONS

COMMENTS
ON ILLUSTRATIONS

1. PLAISANCE BAY (NEWFOUNDLAND).

Early in the seventeenth century, a port of rendezvous was established here by French fishermen. In the foreground are trellises for the drying of fish. The fishing industry is Newfoundland's main economy, and will in all probability continue to be so for a long time to come.

2. CAPELIN FISHING (NEWFOUNDLAND).

The Capelin is a small fish of the Smelt family, abounding all along the Atlantic Coast. In Newfoundland, it is used as food, and also as a fertilizer.

3. PULPWOOD AND NEWSPRINT PLANTS (NEW-FOUNDLAND).

This is the second most important industry in Newfoundland (Pop. 361,416). The annual value of its export trade amounts to more than $ 50,000,000. In the foreground are huge piles of logs destined to be reduced to pulp.

4-5. LOBSTER FISHING (NEWFOUNDLAND).

The lobster is caught in traps like large wooden baskets, with funnel-shaped openings at each end. Attracted by the bait, the shell-fish enters the trap quite readily but then cannot get out. In America, the lobster measures from 24 to 34 inches, including the claws.

6. THE DRYING OF COD (NEWFOUNDLAND).

Cod swarm on the Grand Banks of New-foundland, which were frequented by Norman, Basque and Breton sailors as early as the fourteenth century, if not before. It is the largest fishing ground in the world. The fish are spread on trellises, in the sun, and turned and turned again until completely dried.

7. POTATO FIELD (PRINCE EDWARD ISLAND).

Almost half the total area of Prince Edward Island is under cultivation; the balance is wooded. Agriculture, fishing and fox-ranching comprise the economy of this region, named " Ile Saint Jean " by the French.

8. A BEACH (PRINCE EDWARD ISLAND).

Children and adults come here for amuse-ment. In the distance are sand dunes, swept by the sea at high tide. The Prince Edward Island shores are generally low; the sand is sometimes of a vivid red.

9. CAPE BRETON ISLAND (NOVA SCOTIA).

This island, today a part of Nova Scotia, was formerly called " Ile Royale ", and owing to its strong fortress, Louisbourg, was considered the bulwark of the French Empire in America. The island is famous for its coal deposits.

10. HALIFAX (NOVA SCOTIA).

Founded in 1749 by Lord Edward Corn-wallis, Halifax (Pop. 85,589) is the capital of Nova Scotia (Pop. 642,584). Its harbour is one of the finest in Canada and even in America, and is situated some 600 miles nearer Liverpool than is New York. The harbour is divided into two basins connected by a narrow channel, and covers a total area of over 21 square miles. The water reaches a depth of some 30 feet. Halifax is the terminus of one of the two transcontinental railways.

11. SNOWED-IN VILLAGE (NOVA SCOTIA).

From November to March or April, Eastern Canada is covered with snow. On this white blanket, stretching to the horizon, are some chilly-looking houses clustered around a Church dominating scenery and people alike.

12. APPLE TREES IN BLOOM.

The Annapolis Valley, in Nova Scotia, produces 2,000,000 barrels of apples per year. The first French colony was established in this region in 1604. The greater part of the Acadian population immigrated to New Brunswick. Some 70 to 75,000 inhabitants of French descent or French-speaking still reside in Nova Scotia.

13. A YOKE OF OXEN.

Throughout Canada, especially in the Eastern Provinces where homesteads extend as far as the eye can reach, animal traction has been replaced by machinery. But particularly in the Eastern Provinces there are still a great many farmers who use horses, even yokes of oxen, to carry out their work in the fields.

14. EVANGELINE'S WELL AT GRAND PRÉ (NOVA SCOTIA).

In Longfellow's poem, Evangeline often came to meet her lover, Gabriel, at one of these old wells, the form of which the Acadians of that time had borrowed from their native land. Banished from their villages, the Acadians never returned to the land which they had been the first to conquer. The historical sanctuary of Grand Pré is the only memento of their former presence.

15. FALL PLOUGHING (NOVA SCOTIA).

The land is lush and fertile; it is well worth tilling, yielding a hundredfold. In the distance, below the cliffs, are the dark waters of Minas Basin.

16. A FARM (NOVA SCOTIA).

As none of the farms in this Province are more than 40 miles from the sea, the trees are often swayed by a strong wind coming from the Atlantic.

17. CHESTER REGATTAS (NOVA SCOTIA).

Both young and not-so-young take great interest in these sail-boat races, often highly contested. Wealthy Americans spend the summer at Chester, a very popular vacationland for tourists.

18. A FISHING VILLAGE (NOVA SCOTIA).

The pulley blocks used to unload the barges are hung from gallows, thus lending a lugubrious note to an already grayish and poor-looking landscape. Fishing is one of Nova Scotia's main industries.

19. A FISHING HAVEN (NOVA SCOTIA).

A small harbour sheltered from the wind, like hundreds of others along the scalloped shores of Nova Scotia. In the foreground, a fisherman is on his way to set out his lobster traps about one mile offshore.

20. TROUT FISHING (NOVA SCOTIA).

While commercial fishing is practised all along the coast of Nova Scotia, there is also good sport fishing in all inland lakes, rivers and brooks.

21. A LIGHTHOUSE (NOVA SCOTIA).

Hundreds of lighthouses like this one shed their light over more than 900 miles of coastline, guiding boats, both large and small, to port.

22. THE ANGLICAN CATHEDRAL AT FREDERICTON (NEW BRUNSWICK).

Built from 1845 to 1853, this Cathedral is modelled after St. Mary's Church at Snettisham (England); it is cruciform, with central tower and spire. Fredericton (Pop. 16,018), the capital of New Brunswick, is situated on the west bank of the Saint John River, on the site of the former Acadian village, St. Anne's Point.

23. THE BLESSING OF THE FISHING FLEET (NEW BRUNSWICK).

Each year the blessing of the fishing fleet takes place on a Sunday early in July. It is a French tradition of old Acadia. The French flag is hoisted to the highest mast. The bulk of the French-speaking Acadian population (some 226,000) live in New Brunswick (Pop. 515,697).

24. THE QUEBEC BRIDGE.

An aerial photograph of the Quebec Bridge, rightly called the eighth wonder of the world. It is the longest cantilever span in existence : 1 782 feet. The bridge has a total length of almost two-thirds of a mile, and the metal structure weighs 66,480 tons. While under construction, the arch fell twice : in 1907 and 1916. Finally on September 20, 1917, a third attempt to complete it was crowned with success. This bridge links both banks of the Saint Lawrence and is situated about 7.5 miles west of Quebec.

25. MONTMORENCY FALLS (QUEBEC).

So named by Champlain in 1603, in honour of the Duke of Montmorency, third Viceroy of New France. The Falls are about 250 feet high, but the flow is meagre because of its comparative narrowness (about 53 feet).

26. LOWER TOWN AND QUEBEC HARBOUR (QUEBEC).

This harbour is one of the most sheltered there are. Its wharves can accommodate at least thirty ocean liners at one time. In the centre are the grain elevators, with a capacity of 4,000,000 bushels. Slightly to the right, is seen Laval University, founded in 1852, that originated in the Quebec Seminary, founded in 1663 by the first bishop of New France. The modern University is being built on a large area of land situated at the western limits of the City. In the background are the suburbs : Beauport, Giffard and Courville.

27. THE CHANCEL OF THE BASILICA OF NOTRE DAME (QUEBEC).

In 1640, a first chapel, dedicated to Our Lady of Recovery, was erected on the present site of the Basilica. Ten years later, the first Basilica of Quebec opened its doors to worshippers. In 1744, following successive enlargements, the Basilica attained its present dimensions. Twice destroyed by fire, during the Siege of Quebec and in 1922, it was rebuilt on the same foundations. The canopy and main altar that are shown here were the work of one of the most famous Canadian sculptors, François Baillairgé (1759-1830).

28. A CORRIDOR IN THE URSULINE MONASTERY (QUEBEC).

This is one of the oldest monasteries in North America. Indeed, the Ursulines of Quebec were founded in 1629 by Marie de l'Incarnation. Quebec is the cradle of French civilization on the American continent.

29. THE CHATEAU FRONTENAC HOTEL, AT QUEBEC.

Its main tower overlooks the city. Both its architecture and its name are reminiscent of France in a Province whose motto is " Je me souviens ". A little below the Chateau, is the Post Office. To the left, overlooking the Saint-Lawrence River, is Dufferin Terrace, and the funicular linking it with lowertown.

30. PLAN OF THE CITY OF QUEBEC, IN 1809.

We have very important evidence of what the City of Quebec looked like in the early eighteenth century; it is in the form of a beautiful model to scale, which Jean-Baptiste Duberger, a surveyor with the Royal Engineers, made out of wood between 1805 to 1809; it is preserved in the National Archives, at Ottawa.

31. THE CITADEL OF QUEBEC.

The first fortifications of Quebec date back to Frontenac's second term of office (1693); they have undergone many changes. In the eighteenth century, Levasseur de Néré and Chaussegros de Léry gave them their final form. These army engineers had cherished the dream of crowning Cap Diamond with a citadel " à la Vauban "; it was Elias Walker Durnford, army engineer, who resumed the project in 1820 and erected the Citadel.

32. DES GLACIS STREET, AT QUEBEC.

Quebec (Pop. 164,016) in appearance, seems at times to be an anachronism in the middle of the twentieth century; it is uncommon in all respects, it bears so much the mark of the old world transplanted into the new that its contrast with the other North American cities is as striking as it is instructive.

33. THE TOWER OF THE UNIVERSITY OF MONTREAL (QUEBEC).

This French-speaking University, founded in 1876, and more recently erected on the slopes of Mount Royal, comprises 16 main buildings all linked together, and has a central tower about 265 feet high. The facades stretch just over 900 feet, and the total length of corridors is over 6 miles. This huge building is one of the outstanding models of modern architecture in Canada. There are 14 real universities in Canada, 4 of which are French-speaking and the other 10 English-speaking. The oldest is McGill University (1821) at Montreal.

34. MONTREAL (QUEBEC).

View from the Mount Royal, gradually becoming the centre of the City. In the distance is the Saint Lawrence which is spanned by four bridges : to the right, Victoria Bridge, 1 1/4 miles long. Montreal, situated on the north bank of the St. Lawrence, 1125 miles from the ocean, formerly called Ville-Marie, was founded in 1642 by Jérôme Le Royer and sieur de Maisonneuve. By its population (1,021,520), its trade and its commercial and industrial activity, Montreal may rightly claim the title of Metropolis of Canada. Over three quarters of its inhabitants are French-speaking.

35. MONTREAL TOWARDS 1800 (QUEBEC).

From left to right, one may see Saint Nicholas Gate or Quebec Gate, the steeple of Bon-Secours, the old Citadel and the Jesuits. The city walls which were in ruins at the beginning of the eighteenth century, had been built between 1725 and 1745 by the engineer Gaspard Chaussegros de Léry.

36. THE TOWERS ON THE MOUNTAIN, MONTREAL (QUEBEC).

The Montreal College, which is run by Messieurs de Saint-Sulpice, is one of the oldest institutions of classical education in Canada. Founded in 1767, it was moved less than a century later to the foot of Mount Royal, along the Sherbrooke Street of today, the longest and most elegant of the city's thoroughfares where, at the end of the seventeenth century, stood the Fort de la Montagne. Of this fort two towers remain, one of which was used as a school for some time; they ornament the College gardens.

37. SAINT JOSEPH'S ORATORY, MONTREAL (QUEBEC).

Canada has at least two famous pilgrimage centres, which people come to from all regions of both Americas : Sainte Anne de Beaupré, near Quebec, whose origin dates back to the early stages of the colony, and Saint-Joseph's Oratory, at Montreal, barely half a century old. Its bronze dome and the interior of the nave were designed by Dom Paul Bellot, a renowned Benedictine architect.

38. THE CHURCH OF NOTRE DAME, MONTREAL (QUEBEC).

This Church is one of the most spacious on the North American continent; it was built in 1824, of Gothic style, and is situated in the centre of old Montreal. It is ministered by the Sulpician Fathers, who were the Seigneurs of the Island of Montreal during the French Regime. To the right is the Saint Sulpice Seminary, which dates back to the French Regime (1680). It is surrounded by the business section of the Metropolis of Canada. The Church and Seminary are situated at Place d'Armes, which was the scene of a battle between the French and Iroquois in the early days of the colony. A monument was raised to the memory of Maisonneuve, the founder of Ville Marie, in 1642.

39. CHATEAU DE RAMEZAY, AT MONTREAL (QUEBEC).

This chateau was the residence of Montreal Governors for many years. For the past sixty years it shelters a museum. It was built in 1705 by Pierre Couturier, a master-mason, in honour of Claude de Ramezay, the eleventh Governor of Montreal.

40. PERCÉ AND ITS FAMOUS ROCK (QUEBEC).

This Rock, situated at the far end of the Gaspé Peninsula, was detached from the continent by some prehistorical cataclysm, and offers to the astonished eye the view of an enormous mass of rock, measuring 1,565 feet in length, and its rugged cliff nearly 300 feet high with a cave-like opening, 60 feet high, through which barges may pass at high tide. In the foreground is the village of Percé.

41. BONAVENTURE ISLAND (QUEBEC).

This Island is a bird sanctuary, and is situated 3 miles off the Gaspesian shore. It is the only one of its kind in the world, and is noted for the great variety of species which take refuge there, and live in perfect harmony, and also for the facility with which they may be approached.

42. A FISHING PORT AT GASPÉ (QUEBEC).

Gaspé is an extremely beautiful region, and owing to its varied aspects, it is known as the Brittany of Canada. It was at Gaspé that Jacques Cartier landed on July 24th., 1534. Though poorly endowed, economically, up to these latter years, it is now seeing better days, partly due to a cooperative movement among fishermen. In fact, fishing is the country's main industry, together with the tourist trade.

43. FISHING-BOATS (QUEBEC).

44. MONT SAINT-PIERRE (QUEBEC).

A wooded mountain mass of the Shickshocks group, in Gaspé, mountains that are more ancient than the Rockies. The Gaspesian soil is quite fertile in many regions, but agriculture is only practised to meet essential local requirements. The forest industry is another seasonal employment for the inhabitants, and recent prospecting has revealed that Gaspé's underground conceals important mineral wealth.

45. THE SAINT PIERRE CHURCH (ISLAND OF ORLEANS, QUEBEC).

The Island of Orleans - first called " Ile de Bacchus " by Jacques Cartier - connected with the mainland by a bridge, is situated 18 miles from Quebec. It includes six parishes; some of the oldest houses and churches of the North American continent, excepting Mexico, are located on this Island.

46. A COUNTRY CHURCH (QUEBEC).

47. A PROCESSION CHAPEL (QUEBEC).

As far back as the seventeenth century, it was the custom in New France to build procession chapels in honour of the feast of *Corpus Christi*. That of Neuville, 22 miles from Quebec, on the north shore of the St. Lawrence, built in 1735, is noted for its simple lines and nobleness of proportion.

48. SAINT JEAN PORT JOLI (QUEBEC).

Here and there along both shores of the Saint Lawrence, are villages with French names, of which a great number were founded before the English conquest. A church, presbytery and cemetery form the centre of these peaceful rural communities.

49. THE QUEBEC COUNTRYSIDE (QUEBEC).

This is a typical village of the south shore of the Saint Lawrence : Saint André, County of Kamouraska. The church is one of the most beautiful in the region, and was commenced in 1806. In the offing is Ile des Pèlerins. In the distance, the Laurentians at Saint Siméon on the North Shore.

50. AN OLD CANADIAN HOUSE (QUEBEC).

Especially on the outskirts of Quebec — Island of Orleans and along the Beaupré Coast — there are still a great many old houses which were built in the seventeenth century. Though they were inspired by the style of the houses of the Norman countryside, they are typically " québécoises ".

51. A SNOW-BANKED HOUSE (QUEBEC).

An old Canadian house in rough stone, whitewashed with lime. It is the end of Winter.

52. AN OLD CANADIAN HOUSE (QUEBEC).

The craftsmen who came to Canada during the French Regime had the cult of fine workmanship. Though remaining faithful to the customs they had brought from Normandy and Brittany, they built up a domestic architecture which gave to the countryside of Quebec its special mark of distinction.

53-54-55. OLD CANADIAN HOUSES (QUEBEC).

The old houses of the Quebec countryside, topped with sloping roofs, are more often than not built of large stones and mortar, covered with lime.

56. SEIGNIORIAL MILL AT LES EBOULEMENTS (QUEBEC).

Under the French regime, seigniorial tenure was introduced into Canada. The Seigneurs were essentially paternal, and there was nothing to distinguish them from the common people except the houses they lived in. Very few of these old manors remain; they were very active centres in their day.

57. A WIND MILL (QUEBEC).

An old banal mill, dating back to the French regime. To the right is an old stone house, of Breton style, which is found mostly in the Montreal region; solid and squatty, it is a symbol of resistance.

58. THE THREE MARYS AT THE TOMB ON EASTER MORNING.

In the eighteenth century, New France reckoned a succession of craftsmen, architects and wood carvers : for example, the Levasseurs, the Jourdains dits Labrosse, and the Baillairgés. The Three Marys at the Tomb (1820) carved in wood and enriched with gold, is the masterpiece of the Baillairgés, François and his son Thomas. This work of art can be seen in the Church of Saint Joachim, situated 27 miles from Quebec.

59. "LE BEAU DIEU".

Among the many works that the wood carver, Philippe Liébert (born at Nemours in 1752 and died in Montreal 1804) left, one of the most touching is " Le Beau Dieu ". It is a bas-relief, carved in wood, that adorns the central Tabernacle of the Church of Vaudreuil, 22 miles from Montreal.

60. THE MADONNA.

Of the Levasseur family lineage, Pierre Noël (Quebec 1690-1770) specialized in the carving of statues. In December 1750, at the request of the Jesuit Fathers, he carved an altar-screen for the Chapel of the Congregation, at Quebec. The Madonna in this photograph graced the niche to the left.

61. A TABERNACLE CARVED IN WOOD.

The Canadian school of sculpture included an artisan who was a native of the town of

Avesnes : Gilles Bolvin. From his native Flanders he inherited an exuberant taste for ornamentation, which may easily be seen in the style of the Tabernacle of the Church of Lachenaie, situated 12 miles from Montreal. It is carved in wood, overlaid with gold, and dates back to 1757.

62. THE INTERIOR OF A CHURCH.

An altar-screen of the Recollet type, i. e. in the form of an arch of triumph, may be seen in the Verchères Church 15 miles from Montreal. The entirety is in carved wood and gilded, the work of Louis Quévillon (1818).

63. THE JACK PINE.

The painters who formed, in Toronto, about 1916, the Group of Seven were : Lauren Harris, Alexander Y. Jackson, J.E.H. MacDonald, Arthur Lismer, Frank Johnston, Frank Carmichael, F.H. Varley; later, A.J. Casson joined the Group. In the steps of their forerunner, Tom Thomson (1887-1917), they were ready to resist European influences and they attempted to evolve a purely Canadian School of painting, drawing their inspiration from the northern landscapes. In Thomson's works, we find expressed with a true lyricism the wilderness of Northern Canada.

64. THE SLAVE.

François Beaucourt, a son of the soldier-painter Paul Beaucourt, was born in Laprairie in 1740. He travelled in France, Germany and Russia. After a stay at Bordeaux, where he married the daughter of Camagne, the painter, François Beaucourt returned to Montreal to reside. This reproduction (1786) is a painting of the artist's slave. By the way, slavery never existed in Canada officially, and if there were a few slaves, it was purely accidental.

65. EX-VOTO.

Among the early artists, Canada reckoned one career painter, Claude François, surnamed Brother Luc, a Recollet, born in the town of Amiens, in 1614. Having come to Canada in 1670, he painted religious pieces, and portraits. The Ex-Voto, painted for the Laframboise family (1673), is found in the Church of Saint Philippe, in the City of Trois Rivières.

66. "LA CHASSE AUX TOURTRES" (PASSENGER PIGEONS).

In the work of Antoine Plamondon (1804-1895) religious painting is of little value, but his portrait painting displays skill and a keen sense of honesty. In compositions like " La Chasse aux Tourtres ", he is portrait painting, and furthermore his work is excellent.

67. A STILL LIFE "DOMINOS".

The Canadian school of painting has been flourishing for the past twentyfive years. It is not lacking in boldness of style, as one may easily see in this still life by Alfred Pellan, which hangs in the Provincial Museum, at Quebec.

68. THE GATHERING OF MAPLE WATER (P. OF QUEBEC).

The maple sugar industry is a very ancient one; the richest folklore is closely linked with it. At the first signs of Spring, sugar-making goes through its different phases : the sap or maple water is gathered, reduced to a syrup by means of slight evaporation, and finally the taffy and sugar are produced by the process of higher evaporation. The gathering of the maple sap is a time for merry-making, all of which is staged in the « cabane à sucre ».

69. A MOOSE COMING OUT OF THE WATER.

The Moose, or North American Elk, is king of the Canadian forests. This animal stands 7 feet high at the shoulders, measures 8 feet in length and weighs over 900 pounds. His long and heavy antlers do not hinder in any way his roamings in the depth of the forests, where he moves along with great rapidity. His hearing and sense of smell are acute : he can scent the presence of man at a distance of 2 miles.

70. MOOSE HUNTING.

The great northern regions of Quebec, abounding with lakes, rivers and forests, are excellent hunting grounds. Yet, there are very few who can afford to indulge in this great sport with private plane. In the canoe is a Moose's head with huge antlers.

71. ROD FISHING.

A sport that is much more easy to indulge in, and just as interesting as salmon or speckled trout angling. Youngsters are quite satisfied and happy : " Don't move; I have a bite! "

72. WHEN DAY IS DONE (QUEBEC).

Returning home in a heavy jolting tumbrel, along a road fringing a lake, in which the trees reflect their skeleton branches or dying leaves. This scene was taken on the north bank of the Outaouais River, halfway between Montreal and Ottawa.

73. THE MARKET PLACE (QUEBEC).

Two nuns are doing their early shopping. Most of the important cities of the Province of Quebec (Pop. 4,055,681) have a market place where « habitants » from the neighbouring rural districts come to sell their products.

74. HAYING-TIME (QUEBEC).

The whole family, young and old, men and women, join hands to carry out this work.

75. INTERIOR OF A RURAL HOUSE (QUEBEC).

Almost every rural house has its little industry. The kitchen is the place where the events of everyday life are enacted. Herein, one works, eats and spends long winter evenings, grouped together. During the quiet hours of the afternoon, Granny peacefully winds her wool into a ball.

76. PLOUGHING (ISLAND OF ORLEANS, QUEBEC).

Horses and oxen fraternize in this work.

77. THE BAKING OF BREAD (QUEBEC).

In the homes of a great many Quebec farmers, delicious home-made bread is still baked in open-air ovens, and is eaten with great gusto.

78. BREAD OVEN (QUEBEC).

Among the picturesque structures of the Quebec countryside, the bread oven is worthy of note. There are some of every shape and size. One of the most architectural is the bread oven with a high firechamber, hence those of Saint Jean Port Joli (47 miles from Quebec), on the south shore of the St. Lawrence. The one pictured here is found at St. Philippe (County of Kamouraska) some 16 miles from Saint Jean Port Joli.

79. VAL MORIN (QUEBEC).

A skiing centre situated in the Laurentian Mountains, 45 miles north of Montreal. The Province of Quebec is a great centre of attraction for winter sports fans, Canadians as well as Americans from the North or South.

80. A WATER-FALL IN UNGAVA (QUEBEC).

This uninhabited vast territory, situated to the north-east of the Province of Quebec, is at least twice as extensive as the whole of France. Ungava conceals very rich iron-ore deposits, the development of which has hardly begun. The tiny silhouette of a man standing on the top of the rock to the right, gives one an idea of the size of these falls.

81. THE FLOATING OF LOGS (QUEBEC).

In the springtime when the snow melts and there is an abundance of water, the rivers are the most natural and economical means of transportation for thousands and thousands of tree trunks, cut down each year in the immense forests of Quebec and Ontario. A rough estimate of the value of the forest production in the whole of Canada, amounts to over $ 2,000,000,000 and Quebec produces the lion's share.

82. "LA DRAVE".

The world « drave » comes from the English term " drive "; it is an old popular expression meaning a mass of logs being floated down the rivers, in Canada. These operations are very hazardous and require a lot of courage and skill.

83. HYDRO-ELECTRIC PLANTS (QUEBEC).

The Shawinigan Company, near Three Rivers, is one of the largest hydro-electric plants in Canada; its water power is estimated at nearly 500,000 horse-power. Known hydraulic resources in Canada are 55,000,000 HP. The Province of Quebec alone contains nearly 40 per cent of this amount. So far, Canada is utilizing only 15,000,000 horse-power, a little less than 8,000,000 of which is in the Province of Quebec alone.

84. IN THE RAPIDS.

At times the rafts of timber are halted by an obstacle, and the logs pile up. Dynamite is often used to overcome this blockage, so daring lads depart in canoes to accomplish this work. A century ago, fur traders followed these same " roads that move along ".

85. A PILE OF LOGS.

After having covered a distance of perhaps hundreds of miles, the logs are brought to the mill, and are cut into lengths; they form huge piles that have the appearance of small mountains, and from there they are conveyed to the mill where they are destined to be reduced to wood pulp. Quebec ranks first in the production of wood pulp and newsprint; Ontario comes next.

86. PAPER-MAKING.

A large band of paper (some measuring almost 37 feet in width) comes out of the compressor rolls. If Canada does not rank first in the field of production, it certainly is at least the greatest exporter of paper, especially news-print, with 79 per cent of the total output. This industry comes first in production value (9,900,000 tons, estimated at over $ 950,000,000 dollars in 1954).

87. STEEL-WORKS.

The pouring of steel into ingot-moulds. This method of casting is called bottom-pou-ring. The leading Canadian steelworks are found in Ontario and Quebec; there are even some in Manitoba. The annual output, which amounts to 4,500,000 tons (1954), and is bound to increase from year to year, causes Canada to rank sixth among the steel-producing coun-tries in the world. It would take another 1,000,000 tons for Canada to meet all her requirements.

88. IRON ORE.

In the centre is a mechanical shovel extract-ing the ore, which ore is then loaded on trucks and carted from the mine. The annual pro-duction of iron-ore amounts to 5,300,000 tons (1952). Deposits are found in Ontario and Newfoundland; it is fitting to add those of Quebec : the St. Lawrence North Shore and Ungava.

89. CURLING.

In the wintertime Canadians have the oppor-tunity of indulging in many sports. One of the most popular, among English Canadians especially, is curling. A game developed by the Scots, it is played on ice. The players, provided with brooms, project a heavy stone along a stretch of ice.

90. HOCKEY : A WINTER SPORT.

Hockey is, without a doubt, Canada's nat-ional sport. There is perhaps not a school or a playground which hasn't its skating rink. In large cities, the game is played in vast arenas, before 10,000, 15,000 or 20,000 spectators, comfortably seated. The players wear skates and are armed with a hockey stick, closely resembling a crook, terminating in a curved end. The object of the game is to drive the puck (a vulcanized rubber disc) into the oppo-nent's goal. It requires lightening speed, a quick eye, and strong arms. It often occasions flare-ups amongst the players and spectators.

91. OTTAWA (ONTARIO).

The capital of United Canada in 1857, and ten years later that of Canada. Ottawa (Pop. 202,045) one third or more of whom are French-speaking) is situated on the Ottawa River. In the foreground, along the Rideau Canal, is the railway station and its long platforms. In the centre, the Parliament Buildings, of English Gothic style. On the other side of the river, is the industrial city of Hull (Pop. 43,483), situated in the Province of Quebec.

92. THE PEACE TOWER, OTTAWA (ONTARIO).

The Prince of Wales, who later became Edward VIII, in 1919 laid the corner-stone for this Tower (55 feet high) erected on the facade of the central building of the Parliament of Canada, at Ottawa. This Tower contains, in addition to the big clock, a Memorial Chapel, in honour of all the Canadian soldiers who died at War, and powerful chimes comprising 53 bells, the weight of which varies from 9 pounds to 20,000 pounds.

93. FORT HENRY, AT KINGSTON (ONTARIO)

An historic Fort erected near the emplace-ment where, in 1673, Cavelier de La Salle built Fort Cataraqui, later Fort Frontenac. In the foreground, a sentry on guard. Below, is the Parade Ground. Kingston (Pop. 33,459). situated at the junction of the St. Lawrence River and the Cataraqui, at the eastern inlet of Lake Ontario, is the seat of the Royal Military College and Queen's University.

94. TORONTO (ONTARIO).

The capital of the Province of Ontario (Pop. 4,597,542, of which amount 500,000 are French-speaking), Toronto (Pop. 1,250,000) is the City ranking second as to importance, in Canada. Toronto is the seat of one of the most important universities, and of the largest hotel in the Commonwealth. Each year, an international exhibition is held, whose fame is forever increasing. Toronto extends for some 15 miles along lake Ontario and several miles northwards. Its harbour is a compulsory halting-place for hundreds of cargo vessels plying between the headwaters of Lake Superior, Montreal and Halifax.

95. ON A QUIET LAKE (ONTARIO).

The Province of Ontario, like that of Quebec, includes a great number of lakes of various dimensions, with crystal clear waters, which are favorite summer resorts. Nothing is lacking for an agreeable stay and there are many facilities for sports in addition to beautiful rustic scenery.

96. NIAGARA FALLS (ONTARIO).

They are one of the most spectacular in the world, not so much on account of their height (160 feet) as for their breadth (4,000 feet) and flow (3,000,000 cubic metres per hour). Crowds of tourists come from everywhere to gaze at this marvel; stairways and corridors built in the rock, lead behind the liquid screen. The Falls to the left are on American territory, those to the right, in the form of a horseshoe, are on Canadian soil. They are divided by an island.

97. DEEP IN THE FOREST (ONTARIO).

In quest of game or fish in a bark canoe, a light watercraft which is liable to upset at the least provocation.

98. WELLAND CANAL (ONTARIO).

There is a distance of over 2,300 miles between the Strait of Belle Isle and the headwaters of Lake Superior. West of Montreal canals had to be built in order to pass from one lake to another, and avoid waterfalls or rapids. The Welland Canal, whose construction dates back to 1829, facilitates passage between Lake Erie and Lake Ontario, permitting avoidance of the insurmountable obstacle of the Niagara Falls and River.

99. FORT WILLIAM (ONTARIO).

This is a twin city to Port Arthur, also renowned for its grain elevators. The population is 34,947.

100. THE PRAIRIES (MANITOBA).

One of the central provinces, called the Prairies Provinces. In prehistoric times these plains were covered with a sheet of water. When the waters receded, there remained alluvium deposits which resulted in very fertile land. Plant growth is very rapid.

101. A SAUTEUX CHIEF.

The Ojibwa or Sauteux Indians are strong and jovial types, of fine physique, proud and brave. They are the largest tribe in Canada; the majority inhabit the region of the Great Lakes.

102. AN ALGONQUIN AND HER BABY.

The Algonquin race, one of the chief native tribes of the country, (by now has dwindled down to a few thousand), were driven towards the north or quartered in special reservations. Altogether, Canada numbers nearly 13,7000 Indians and some 10,000 Eskimos.

There are also about 36,000 half-breeds, of whom more than 8,000 are French-speaking : the others speak a mixed dialect of English and Indian.

103. A FARM IN MANITOBA.

In this Province, called the granary of Canada, the principal crop is wheat, a very superior quality of wheat, produced by a fertile soil, and improved by scientific selection. Together with Alberta and Saskatchewan, Manitoba contributes towards giving Canada her rank as second wheat-producing country in the world (688,000,000 bushels in 1952), and first in the wheat export trade (304,700,000 bushels in 1952). Production in 1951 (562,398,000 bushels) was slightly inferior to the crop of 1928 which exceeded 566,000,000 bushels. In 1954, it dropped to 513,000,000 bushels.

104. DUCK-HUNTING (MANITOBA).

The swamps of Manitoba abound with wild duck, and hunters too.

105. THE WINNIPEG RIVER (MANITOBA).

Both Winnipeg Lake and River — Winnipeg being an Indian word meaning " muddy water " — are well stocked with fish, though the river's course is rugged, broken by rapids and waterfalls. The capital of the Province of Manitoba (Pop. 776,541, of whom 60,000 are French-speaking and at least as many are Ukranians), situated at the confluence of the Red and Assiniboine Rivers, it also bears the name of Winnipeg (Pop. 233,710). It was here that La Vérendrye built Fort Rouge in 1738.

106. SASKATOON (SASKATCHEWAN).

Saskatoon, the second largest city of Saskatchewan (which comes from the Indian word " Missikatchewan " meaning " swift current "), is situated on the River bearing the same name. This city, covering an area of 21.5 square miles, is a mushroom city like many other Western cities. It was really founded in 1885. Today, with a population of 53,268 inhabitants, it is an important railroad and business centre. Owing to its geographical position it is also a distributing and forwarding point for the products of a vast agricultural area. There are grain elevators with a storage capacity of 5,000,000 bushels. The population of Saskatchewan is 829,175, of whom 50,000 are French-speaking. The capital is Regina (Pop. 71,319); it was founded by a group of French Canadians in 1882.

107. A FARM (SASKATCHEWAN).

The house and outbuildings are surrounded by a screen of trees, that serves as a protection against the wind, and to hide the monotonous view of the vast plains. To the right, is a private plane. Saskatchewan is mainly an agricultural region : grain-growing and raising of live-stock. Like other Western Provinces its population has increased rapidly owing to the influx of immigrants from Eastern Canada and Europe.

108-109. THE HARVEST (ALBERTA).

The broad Western plains are already merging into the foothills. In the foreground, is a scythe; in the distance are wheat fields alternating with those of buckwheat. Alberta (Pop. 939,501, of whom 56,185 are French-Canadians) is the Canadian Province where colonization has advanced farthest northwards. While remaining an agricultural Province and an important cattle-breeding area, it has tended to become greatly industrialized since the recent discovery of oil, gas and coal deposits.

110. WATER TRANSPORT (ALBERTA).

In the northern part of the Province where railroads are less developed, the rivers are an indispensable means of communication during five or six months of the year.

111. OIL-WELLS (ALBERTA).

The number of oil-wells in Alberta is greatly on the increase, especially in the neighbourhood of Edmonton (Pop. 159,631), the capital of the Province, founded less than a century ago. Oil production in Alberta, constantly increasing, today supplies onethird of Canada's requirements. A pipeline, the construction of which had been completed in 1951, conveys crude oil as far as Sarnia (Ontario), that is a distance of 1,765 miles, and an other one to Vancouver on the Pacific (718 miles).

112. THE CALGARY-BANFF HIGHWAY (ALBERTA).

This excellent route enables one to cross the Rockies from Calgary, important city in the south of Alberta (Pop. 129,060), to Vancouver. This route passes through Banff. It winds uphill unceasingly, at times through deep valleys, and at other times along the brow of high cliffs.

113. A TRAIN IN THE ROCKIES (ALBERTA).

Even the railroad, built, it is true, at the cost of millions, succeeded in winding its way across the gigantic mountains. Here is a Canadian Pacific train puffing its way up an incline, at times very steep. Farther north runs the Canadian National Railways line that crosses the Rockies between Edmonton and the Pacific Coast, through Jasper, a vacation-land for tourists especially in summertime, but also during winter, though then the larger hotels are closed.

114. THE TOWN OF BANFF (ALBERTA).

Situated in the Rocky Mountains, 80 miles from Calgary. A small centre of 2,357 inhabitants. It is a rendezvous for tourists, attracted by the mountains, glaciers, forests, lakes and hot sulphur springs.

115. THE BANFF SPRINGS HOTEL (ALBERTA).

The Canadian Pacific Company has built one of its most luxurious hotels in the midst of this majestic scenery.

116. MORAINE LAKE (ALBERTA).

This is one of the many, and also one of the most beautiful lakes, in the Rockies, and is fed by glaciers. Compared with these masses of rock, the tall pine trees seem like so many matches.

117. MALIGNE LAKE (ALBERTA).

One of the gorgeous lakes of Jasper Park in the northern Rockies. It measures over 30 miles in length and is named after the Maligne River, into which it discharges.

118. A LAKE IN THE ROCKIES.

119. IN THE ROCKIES (BRITISH COLUMBIA).

Slopes are not lacking and the tourists are well aware of it, for they come in droves each year.

120. THE GREAT DIVIDE (ALBERTA AND BRITISH COLUMBIA).

This is the watershed and at the same time the border between the Provinces of Alberta and British Columbia. This picture was taken from the British Columbia side looking towards Alberta. The altitude of the highway at this point is over 5,000 feet.

121. JERVIS COVE (BRITISH COLUMBIA).

The coast of British Columbia is indented by a multitude of fjords like this one, thrusting in between high banks.

122. A RIVER (BRITISH COLUMBIA).

123. A FLOCK OF SHEEP (BRITISH COLUMBIA).

On the Columbian Plateau, between the Rockies and the shore Mountains, there is excellent pasture-land or grazing ground, where breeding of live-stock is practised on a large scale.

124. TOTEM POLES (BRITISH COLUMBIA).

It is chiefly in British Columbia that native tribes practice Totemism. The Totems are great fir tree-trunks on which symbolic figures of men, birds, or animals are carved, and enhanced with brilliant colours. The order in which they are arranged and their symbolic nature are indicative of a certain hierarchy of the ancestors of each clan or tribe, and also of family history.

125. AN ORCHARD (BRITISH COLUMBIA).

The southern part of British Columbia and the prairies rolling between the mountains and the sea, enjoys a very mild climate. Fruit-growing is practised intensively, apples being particularly famous for their high quality. To the right is Lake Okanagan.

126. VANCOUVER (BRITISH COLUMBIA).

One of the finest harbours of Canada open the year round, and gateway to the Far East, the City of Vancouver (Pop. 344,833) ranks third in Canada after Montreal and Toronto. British Columbia (Pop. 1,165,210, of whom at least 40,000 are French-speaking), abounding in mineral wealth and precious metals, has undergone intense industrial development during the past few years.

127. FISHING-BOATS (BRITISH COLUMBIA).

They crowd Vancouver Harbour, while waiting to put out to sea.

128. SALMON FISHING (BRITISH COLUMBIA).

Fishing is another important source of revenue for British Columbia. Salmon in particular abounds in the many fjords along the coast of this Province. Seining is the method employed for salmon.

129. VICTORIA (BRITISH COLUMBIA).

The capital of British Columbia, situated at the southern end of Vancouver Island on the Strait of Juan de Fuca, Victoria (Pop. 51,331) was founded in 1843. It is the site of the astrophysical and meteorological observatories of the Canadian Government; there is also a beautiful botanical garden. The climate is uncommonly temperate. In the centre, the inner harbour.

130. A BEACH (BRITISH COLUMBIA).

Near Banfield, on the west coast of Vancouver Island, therefore at the most westerly point of Canada, on the Pacific Ocean. The water is heated by the Kouro-Sivo; but watch out for the breakers!

131. FLYING.

Of late years, airplane-building in Canada has made incredible strides. The same may be applied to its air-lines which have multiplied. There are few places in Canada, either East or West, as well as North or South, which cannot be reached by air. Naturally, there also exist regular plane services between Canada and Europe and Asia, and even one that links Edmonton with Copenhagen via the North Pole.

The illustrations in this volume have been furnished by :

AIR-CANADA *for plates* 103, 106 *and* 131.

ASSOCIATED SCREEN NEWS LTD (MONTREAL) *for plates* 14, 34, 37 *and* 92.

NOVA SCOTIA BUREAU OF INFORMATION *for plates* 10, 13, 15, 16, 17, 19, 20 *and* 21.

NEW BRUNSWICK BUREAU OF INFORMATION *for plates* 22 *and* 23.

CANADIAN GOVERNMENT TRAVEL BUREAU *for plate* 116.

BRITISH COLUMBIA GOVERNMENT TRAVEL BUREAU *for plates* 118, 120, 121, 122, 129 *and* 130.

RAYMOND CARON (MONTREAL) *for plates* 71 *and* 72.

CANADIAN NATIONAL RAILWAYS *for plates* 1, 2 *and* 6.

CANADIAN PACIFIC RAILWAY *for plates* 11, 18, 57, 70, 73, 85, 97, 108, 109, 111, 113, 114 *and* 127.

THE SHAWINIGAN WATER AND POWER COMPANY *for plates* 83.

L'INVENTAIRE DES ŒUVRES D'ART (QUEBEC) *for plates* 30, 31, 35, 47, 49, 58, 59, 60, 61, 62, 63, 64, 65, 66, 67 *and* 78.

KORO PHOTOS REG'D (MONTREAL) *for plate* 36.

ARMOUR LANDRY (MONTREAL) *for plates* 38 *and* 39.

LOUIS LANOUETTE (QUEBEC) *for plates* 24, 25, 26 *and* 90.

ONTARIO DEPARTMENT OF TRAVEL AND PUBLICITY *for plates* 69, 89, 95, 98, 99 *and* 101.

NATIONAL FILM BOARD (OTTAWA) *for plates* 3, 4, 5, 7, 8, 9, 12, 80, 86, 87, 88, 93, 96, 107, 115, 117, 119, 123, 124, 125 *and* 128.

PROVINCE OF QUEBEC TOURIST BUREAU *Driscoll Photos for plates* 27, 28, 29, 33, 40, 41, 42, 46, 51, 68, 74, 75, 76, 77 *and* 102.

OMER PARENT (QUEBEC) *for plates* 32, 43, 44, 45, 48, 50, 52, 53, 54, 55 *and* 56.

PHOTOGRAPHIC SURVEYS CORPORATION (TORONTO) *for plates* 91, 94 *and* 126.

BUREAU OF TRAVEL AND PUBLICITY (MANITOBA) *for plates* 100, 104 *and* 105.

PHOTOGRAPHY BUREAU OF ALBERTA *for plates* 110 *and* 112.

STUDIO MALAK (OTTAWA) *for plates* 81, 82 *and* 84.

SUN VALLEY FARM *for plate* 79.

This volume, in the series
" WONDERS OF FRANCE
AND OF THE WORLD ",
has been produced on the
presses of
Théo BRUGIÈRE
Malakoff (Seine)

PRINTED IN FRANCE

Date Due